Listening
The Forgotten Skill

Wiley Self-Teaching Guides teach practical skills from accounting to astronomy, management to mathematics. Look for them at your local bookstore.

Other Wiley Self-Teaching Guides on Business Skills:

Accounting: A Self-Teaching Guide, by Neal Margolis and N. Paul Harmon

Effective Meetings: A Self-Teaching Guide, by Clyde W. Burleson

Making Successful Presentations: A Self-Teaching Guide, by Terry C. Smith

Managing Assertively: A Self-Teaching Guide, Second Edition, by Madelyn Burley-Allen

Managing Behavior on the Job: A Self-Teaching Guide, by Paul L. Brown

Quick Business Math: A Self-Teaching Guide, by Steve Slavin

Selling on the Phone: A Self-Teaching Guide, by James Porterfield

Successful Time Management: A Self-Teaching Guide, Second Edition, by Jack D. Ferner

Listening
The Forgotten Skill

A Self-Teaching Guide

Second Edition

Madelyn Burley-Allen

John Wiley & Sons, Inc.

New York • Chichester • Brisbane • Toronto • Singapore

Copyright © 1995 by Madelyn Burley-Allen
Published by John Wiley & Sons, Inc.

Library of Congress Cataloging-in-Publication Data:

Burley-Allen, Madelyn.
    Listening : the forgotten skill / Madelyn Burley-Allen. — 2nd ed.
        p.   cm. — (A self-teaching guide)
    Includes bibliographical references and index.
    ISBN 0-471-01587-3 (pbk.)
    1. Listening. I. Title. II. Series.
BF323.L5B87   1995
650.1′3—dc20   94-33343

Printed in the United States of America

15 14 13

Contents

Preface

When I wrote the first edition of this book in 1982, I had been involved in the beginnings of the "listening movement" for 11 years. You might be wondering why I refer to listening in this way.

Because of the value and benefits of listening, the interest in listening has been sweeping America. The information revolution has forced us all to develop ways to cope with massive loads of data. We first need to sort out what's really being said. The accelerated pace with which information is exchanged between people within organizations demands that people listen effectively so mistakes aren't made, misunderstandings and misinterpretations are avoided.

In the early 1980s many companies would have laughed off listening training. The assumption was that everyone is born to listen effectively—if you hear, you can listen. Today, however, many Fortune 500 businesses now believe that human problems they once dismissed as irrelevant to profitability do affect the bottom line. On nearly every company's list of human problems is communication. Sperry Corporation made a name for itself as the company that listens.

Many of my customers have made listening a basic part of their management philosophy. They have found out that better listening means that people are more open to new ideas, and there is more innovation and better customer service, as sales and design staff pay attention to customer needs. In addition, good listening can reduce stress, avoid conflict, and assist customer representatives in handling difficult people more effectively. When you realize that 45 percent of people's time is spent listening, you can understand why effective listening is so vital. Effective listening becomes even more critical as one moves up the corporation ladder: The percentage of time increases to 55 percent. An article describing the richest 15 Americans asked each of them the question, "Is it possible for anyone to become America's richest?" The millionaires and billionaires say yes. Among their suggestions: Be a good listener, do it yourself, establish a good relationship with a bank and borrow.

My research shows a two-day listening seminar impacts participants in a variety of ways. The data was processed by the New West Research Corporation, Stanford, California, by giving each participant a pre-seminar questionnaire and following up eight weeks later, after the completion of training, with a post-seminar questionnaire. The following results were scores obtained from a yearly random sample of participants of my "listening" seminar.

1. Value of the Seminar to Job Performance

   Eighty percent of the participants rated the seminar as valuable to their job performance.

2. Seminar Impact Measures

   As a result of participating in the seminar:

   Eighty-three percent of the participants reported understanding the listening process more clearly.

   Eighty-five percent of the participants increased their level of awareness on what they do that interferes with their listening.

   Eighty percent of the participants reported that they listen to others more openly.

   Seventy-five percent of the participants reported having better understanding of their listening habits.

   Seventy-two percent of the participants reported that their communication with others has improved.

   Seventy-eight percent of the participants reported improved understanding of self and others.

   Forty-eight percent of the participants are more satisfied with their jobs.

   Sixty-eight percent of the participants reported that they are more effective in handling difficult people.

   Fifty-three percent of the participants reported increased effectiveness on the job.

3. Areas of Personal Improvement

   A. *Personal Awareness*   Seventy percent of the participants reported improvement.

B. *Conceptual Awareness*   Seventy-one percent of the participants reported improvement.

C. *Acceptance of Ideas of Skills Needed*   Seventy-two percent of the participants reported improvement.

D. *Utilization of Remedies and Internalization of Behavior*   Sixty-eight percent of the participants reported improvement.

E. *Integration Measures*   Fifty-eight percent of the participants reported improvement.

This research data confirms that many companies have learned to incorporate listening training as part of their core curriculum. Listening training has a variety of positive effects that could be equated to the bottom line.

The intention of the material in this book is to help you gain the benefits mentioned above by improving your listening abilities.

I will be sharing with you approaches I found that increased my self-confidence, thereby improving my ability to handle conflict, solve problems, and relieve stress and tension in both business and personal relationships. During the past 22 years of conducting "listening" seminars, I have found that people respond positively to empathetic listeners because people have a deep need to be listened to. Effective listeners know how to obtain the information and results they seek.

One of my goals in writing this book was to assist you, the reader, in breaking down your barriers to listening, barriers that interfere with positive relationships. The examples and exercises throughout the book were developed to lead you through skill development that will allow you to make effective changes in your listening behavior. Many of these same exercises are used in the seminars I conduct.

This book is a part of a journey I have taken to discover myself and to study how my relationships with others could be improved. The journey was motivated by a personal tragedy that led me to question who I was and what I was. Because of this tragedy, I pursued various avenues to understand myself. The books and authors listed in the suggested reading list were some of those avenues, avenues that moved me toward the process of listening to how I was talking both to myself and others.

While I was moving through this self-discovery, my profession changed. Where I had once been dealing in the business world, I was now involved with applied psychology and designing workshops in communication and skill building. During my seminars, people would often say that they didn't feel listened to and that they felt that most people didn't listen well—including themselves.

The necessity of developing a seminar that specifically dealt with improving listening habits became more and more obvious to me. This decision resulted in years of research and testing, and finally, in application in seminars.

Often, people in my seminars would say, "I've learned so much in your course that is useful. Why don't you write a book about it?" Although I found verbalizing what I had learned easy and natural, the thought of writing it in book form was downright scary. Writing seemed so final. After all, when you say something that isn't worthwhile, there is a good chance that the person you said it to wasn't listening or certainly would forget what was said. But, with writing, people could always go back and read it again—quite a risk. However, the urging of those attending my seminars motivated me to go through the struggle of writing down what I found so easy to verbalize.

My hope is that the material in this book will help you as much as it helped me in my journey toward self-improvement.

Madelyn Burley-Allen

Acknowledgments

I gratefully acknowledge all of the ideas regarding listening behavior that were shared with me by the individuals attending my seminars throughout the past 25 years. Their input has sharpened the material and enhanced the examples used in this book.

The concepts and format of this book have been discussed at length with colleagues Betty Burr, Kristin Anundsen, Lloyd Smigle, and Robert A. Rickert, Jr. Their assistance in developing the format and the focus of the material have contributed much to the clarity of the book.

I wish to thank all of the talented people with whom I have studied and worked. I especially appreciate being associated with and having learned from Dorothy Jongeward, Ph.D., Bernard Dohrmann, and the training staff on Thomas Gordon's Effectiveness Training Institute. The writings of Eric Berne, M.D., Frederick Perls, M.D., Bhagwan Shree Rajneesh, Albert Ellis, Ph.D., Jack Canfield, and William Glasser have been most nourishing and meaningful to me.

Many institutions aided in the development of my listening program that led to this book, most particularly the training centers of the Office of Personnel Management in San Francisco and Seattle. A most special thanks goes to Jean Mizuiri and Leise Robbins for giving me the opportunity to develop and conduct numerous listening seminars, which served as the foundation of this book. Finally, I acknowledge the hard work done by my dedicated assistants, Dorothy Sipple, Faye Klein, and Judith Buchanan, who helped make this book possible by getting the vast amount of typing completed for publication.

For information about a complete prepackaged listening program and other listening products, write or call:

Dynamics of Human Behavior
P.O. Box 2344
Wimberley, Texas 78676
Phone (512) 847–0595
Fax (512) 847–0597
Web www.dynamics-hb.com
E-mail dhb8@hooked.net

1

What Is Listening and What Can It Do for You?

Speech is a joint game between the talker and the listener against the forces of confusion. Unless both make the effort, interpersonal communication is quite hopeless.

Norbert Weiner,
"The Human Use of Human Beings"

"I was astounded! All I had to do was listen, and this employee of mine worked through his own problem without me giving a bit of advice."

This comment was made by a man on the second day of a listening skills seminar. Newly aware of his own listening patterns, he stopped himself from jumping in with solutions when an employee began sharing a problem. Instead, he listened quietly and occasionally paraphrased what he was being told. The employee came to his own conclusions right there in front of him. "I realized how much I had been interfering with allowing others to build their confidence by being too quick to give advice," he continued. "I was amazed that most people just wanted me to listen to them."

Statements from others who have completed listening skills training include:

> "My communication is more real, meaningful, worthwhile, and at a deeper level."
> "I've cleared up some problems I was having at work."
> "I'm more honest with myself now."
> "I can refrain from interrupting."
> "I think I am a better supervisor because I now hear beyond the spoken words."

These remarks indicate a definite connection between listening skills, improved interpersonal communication, professional growth, and career satisfaction. For example, if you're a skilled listener, more people will respond to you in a positive way. You can sell yourself in job interviews, cut down your problem-solving time, and smooth out work relationships. People will respond to you more favorably in any situation.

This may surprise you because the idea of listening as a "skill" is unfamiliar. Communication as a "skill" is a common enough concept. Yet, of all the time we spend communication, *by far the greatest is spent in listening* (see Figure 1.1).

Here's how the communication process breaks down.[1]

You may not have realized listening is such an important, yet often overlooked or seriously short-changed, skill in many business activities—even though we spend 70 percent of our waking hours in verbal communication.

A manager who was curious about how much time he spent listen-

FIGURE 1.1

A breakdown of the time we spend on each aspect of the communication process.

40%   Listening
35%   Talking
16%   Reading
9%   Writing

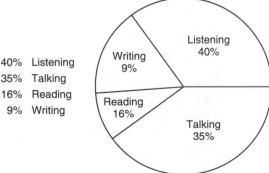

ing asked his secretary to keep track of the time he spent on the telephone, listening. He was shocked to discover his company was paying him 35–40 percent of his salary, or $18,000, for this function alone.

Amazingly, on the average, people are only about 25 percent effective as listeners. If this manager's listening skill is at that 25 percent efficiency rate, about $13,500 is paid for time he spends listening ineffectively.

Listening as a method of taking in information is used far more than reading and writing combined. It is the channel used most often for learning. Ironically, it is the least understood function of all. When we think about listening, we tend to assume it is basically the same as hearing; this is a dangerous misconception because it leads us to believe effective listening is instinctive. As a result, we make little effort to learn or develop listening skills and unknowingly neglect a vital communication function, thereby denying ourselves educational development and increased self-awareness.

Consequently, we create unnecessary problems for ourselves: misunderstandings, hurt feelings, confused instructions, loss of important information, embarrassment, and frustration. We lose the opportunity to improve our professional and personal relationships.

Listening involves a more sophisticated mental process than hearing. It demands energy and discipline. Listening is a learned skill. The first step is to realize that effective listening is an *active,* not a passive, process. This is a difficult concept, but it is true: A skilled listener does not just sit there and allow listening to happen.

What *is* listening, then? One way to answer this question is to ask two other questions:

- What does it feel like to really listen to someone else?

- What does it feel like when someone really listens to you?

The answers to these questions provide a definition of effective listening, one on which this book is based:

> Listening is (a) taking in information from speakers, other people or ourselves, while remaining nonjudgmental and empathetic; (b) acknowledging the talker in a way that invites the communication to continue; and (c) providing limited, but encouraging, input to the talker's response, carrying the person's idea one step forward. This definition stresses the listener's responsibility in the communication process. Although listening is one of the most demanding aspects of communication, it is also one of the most rewarding.

RELATIONSHIPS

A supervisor related this incident involving herself and an employee:

It was one of those days when three major projects were due. The supervisor, Janet, felt harried and tense as she completed the most important project, a financial report. Suddenly, an employee, Jeff, appeared at the front door looking distraught. "Janet," he said, "We can't go any further with this report. I misplaced the project summary statements!"

Janet's first impulse as a supervisor was to snap, "What! Can't you do anything right?" Instead, she stopped what she was doing, took a deep breath, and gave him her full attention.

"Hmmm, tell me what you have already done to find the statements," she said.

"First," began Jeff, "I asked Dave if he had them. He remembered giving them to me yesterday before he left work. Then I remembered putting them on my desk with a note for Dana to type them this morning. Dana told me she returned them for my review just before lunch."

"So you tracked them down until lunch time," responded Janet. "What happened next?"

"That's where I draw a blank! I just can't remember what I did with them next!"

"Jeff," replied Janet, "I can see you're really upset about this."

"Yes, I am. It's not like me to misplace something like this."

"Well," continued Janet, "Let's sit down a minute. Perhaps if you close your eyes and see yourself getting the statements from Dana, you might come up with what you did next. Just relax and see what happens."

Jeff sat there, eyes closed, for almost three minutes. Suddenly his face lit up, he opened his eyes and exclaimed, "I remember now! Joe brought me the Jensen report when I had the financial statements in my hand. I bet they're under that report!" Jeff checked, and sure enough, the financial statements were right where he thought they would be.

By listening with understanding and remaining objective, Janet helped Jeff stay calm and solve the mystery of the misplaced statements himself. This interaction helped Janet develop a positive working relationship with her staff. She interpreted it as one of the most important ingredients of her success as a boss.

What happened between Janet and Jeff is illustrated by the diagram in Figure 1.2.

Jeff's emotional level was high when he walked into Janet's office. As Janet effectively listened to Jeff, without getting upset herself or judging his behavior as "bad," his emotional level was lowered. By reducing his level of emotion, Jeff was then able to think his problems through.

Listening as a way to acknowledge someone often increases self-esteem. It is a way of saying to the talker, "You are important, and I am not judging you." That is why listening is such a powerful force in human relationships.

In turn, people who are being listened to usually appreciate the people who are doing the listening and cooperate with them. Why? Acknowledgment is a basic, universal, human need. We are more likely to respond positively to a person who meets these needs than to one who does not.

Listening is a potent force for reducing stress and tension. True listening builds teamwork, trust, and a sense of belonging to a group. When people know they are talking to a listener instead of someone who sits in judgment, they openly suggest ideas and share thoughts. The listener then has an opportunity to respond to the person's concerns and needs that otherwise might have gone unnoticed.

FIGURE 1.2
Effective listening to an emotional person.

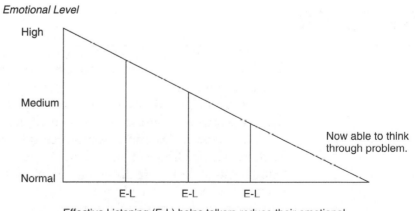

Effective Listening (E-L) helps talkers reduce their emotional level so they can think the problem through.

The listener sets in motion a positive, mutually rewarding process by demonstrating interest in both the talker and what the talker says. The talker feels more accepted and gives more valid information. The listener asks more relevant questions. This empathetic listening encourages honesty, understanding, and a feeling of security.

Listening also encourages people to feel self-confident. For example, when co-workers share their problems, do you get the sinking feeling it is your responsibility to solve them? If so, you are probably wasting your energy. A request for listening is usually not a request for giving advice. It is a request to be listened to nonjudgmentally, from the heart.

Your act of listening is the only help required. Active listening alleviates a problem by giving the person a chance to talk it through while experiencing emotional release and at the same time providing limited and empathetic input that conveys to the talker your concern and nonjudgmental attitude—as occurred in the example of the employee who lost the project summary statements. Given the opportunity to solve their own problems, people tend to feel more confident in their abilities.

Employees who are listened to will not bottle up their feelings. Listening tells the employee, "Your feelings are legitimate." Employees who are not listened to get the message that their feelings are not important. Holding feelings in does not get rid of them. Sooner or later they will erupt. When they do, it will probably be in a negative way, such as missing deadlines, being late for work, or not putting in the extra effort to get a job done.

SELF-AWARENESS

Effective listening involves not only tuning in to others, but tuning in to ourselves. Listening carefully to *what* we say and how we say it can teach us an immense amount about ourselves.

For example, if we know how to listen to ourselves, we will discover the key words and phrases we repeatedly use. For many of us, one such word is "should." Suppose you notice that you often say, "I should go back to school and get my M.A. degree." You might ask, "Is that 'should' something I really want for myself, or is it what my parents wanted for me? What will *I* get out of it?" In examining these questions, you begin to determine whether you do things of your *own* choice or that of someone else. This kind of awareness brings you closer to being "the chooser."

Statements we make about ourselves or others reflect our own self-concept, our thought patterns, and our belief systems. If, for example, you heard yourself making the following statements, what would you learn about yourself?

"I'm not very artistic—can't draw a straight line with a ruler."
"I can't get a promotion—I don't have a degree."
"I can't get to anything on time."
"I'd like to tell my boss how I feel, but I can't."
"Someday I'm going to find time to get organized."
"I can't handle angry people."

Take a moment to reflect on these statements and note here what you have learned from them:

As we'll see in Chapter 4, self-awareness grows as we discover *how* we communicate. Consequently this increases our ability to interrelate with others. Listening to oneself is a basic step toward professional growth and development.

PROFESSIONAL DEVELOPMENT AND SUCCESS

The movement toward professional success began in school, where we learned concepts and behaviors to help us achieve what we want. In school, we spent most of our time taking in information by reading or listening.

Sara W. Lundsteen, a specialist in classroom listening, points out that the earliest language skill to appear is listening. She adds that "reading may depend so completely upon listening as to appear to be a special extension of listening. What child does not read a selection better after listening and talking about it? . . . The ability to listen seems to set limits on the ability to read."[2]

Improving how we listen in class often means better grades. Better grades mean our self-concept will move up a notch or two. People who have completed my listening skills workshops often say they feel better about themselves. Not only have they deepened their self-awareness, they have also sharpened a skill they know will be useful in personal and professional development.

On the job, an effective listener has a significant edge over those who are not. A study conducted by Loyola University researchers sought the answer to the question, What is the single most important attribute of an effective manager? Thousands of workers were questioned, with the results summarized as follows:

> Of all the sources of information a manager has by which he can come to know and accurately size up the personalities of the people in his department, listening to the individual employee is the most important. The most stereotyped report that we have received from thousands of workers who testified that they like their supervisor was this one: "I like my boss, he listens to me, I can talk to him."

Bosses who listen earn the respect and loyalty of their staff. They discover important things about how the business is going. One company hired an expensive management consultant to find out why workers showed signs of low morale. The consultant began searching for the cause of dissatisfaction using a method the company's managers could have used themselves. He directly asked the workers why they were unhappy—and listened to their answers.

Employees frequently have excellent ideas about improving productivity of the work environment. Managers who listen for these ideas solve more problems than those who do not. These managers create a sense of concern for their staff while receiving better-quality information.

A foreman reported the following listening encounter that he experienced with one of his supervisors.

> One day Dave, the foreman, called the supervisor, José, into his office to explain his plans for a new way to assemble machinery. He described how he thought the procedure should be changed. José's only response was silence and a frown. The foreman realized something was wrong and sensed José might have something to say.
>
> "José," he began, "You've been in the department longer than me. What's your reaction to my suggestion? I'm listening."

José paused and then began to speak. He realized Dave had opened the door to communication and felt comfortable offering suggestions from his years of experience.

As the two employees exchanged ideas, a mutual respect and trust developed, along with a solution to the technical problems. While listening, Dave remained in complete control of the situation. He was an active, not a passive, listener.

A manager who listens encourages employee growth and career development. One manager consistently asked his staff what they wanted from their careers. Some had never given it much thought. However, once they had his empathetic ear and felt his support, they developed some well-thought-out career plans. The manager listened carefully to what each employee said. First, he asked questions to confirm that he understood what they had in mind. Then, based on his years in the business, he told them what career opportunities were available in the company. In each case, he suggested people to contact and how to prepare a step-by-step plan for moving up. After making suggestions, he listened again for a response to gauge the appropriateness of his recommendations. All involved in this listening process expanded their awareness. The effects rippled outward like waves. The employees progressed faster in their careers than others in the company, and the company benefited substantially. These employees produced more work and contributed more useful ideas.

It is amazing that any organization can operate with a low level of listening efficiency. Imagine the possible growth in productivity if listening effectiveness were doubled, tripled, or quadrupled!

No matter what our area of business, listening improves our effectiveness. We get more accomplished. A great deal of business activity involves selling: selling a product, an idea, or ourselves. Any sales training course devotes significant time to developing listening skills. Sales people who listen get the sales. A successful salesperson has learned to listen for the needs of the prospects and then to respond by meeting those needs.

For example, a salesperson trying to sell a new car might ask a prospect, "Where do you normally drive?" If the person replies, "Between Los Angeles and Phoenix," the salesperson might say, "You drive a lot in hot climates. You probably need a car that performs well in high temperatures, don't you?" When the prospect mentioned something she considered desirable, the salesperson had a perfect chance to respond by mentioning how his brand of car fulfilled that requirement.

In contrast is the sales clerk who was asked by a customer for a particular sweater in green. The clerk brought out a blue one. When the customer reminded the clerk she asked for green, the clerk replied, "Oh, it doesn't come in green. The manufacturer doesn't make it in that color because there's no call for it." Imagine how the customer felt. By not listening, the clerk first ignored the customer and then insulted her. That was probably the last time the customer would deal with that clerk.

PRACTICE SESSION

This session is designed to help you start becoming aware of your listening efficiency. Select a person you feel comfortable with and ask that person to do a listening check when the two of you are talking.

This listening check involves your summarizing what you think was said after the person has completed a thought or idea. By forcing yourself to summarize what was said, you will become aware of how well you listen. If you cannot summarize, examine what you do that keeps your listening efficiency low. It usually means you have been doing some internal process, such as daydreaming, going on mental tangents, or forming a rebuttal. Over a period of time, listening practice should help you to improve your listening efficiency.

EXERCISE 1.1

Let's explore situations in your organization that will help sharpen your ability to identify ways nonlistening occurs:

1. What examples of ineffective listening have you seen in your organization? Describe the situations. What could have been done so that the situations didn't happen?

2. List the ways in which more effective listening could benefit your organization (performance appraisal, listening to criticism, listening to an emotional customer, etc.).

3. Think of a person in your organization whom you consider an effective listener. How do you feel when you talk to this person?

LISTENING AND INTERPERSONAL POWER

We can use listening skills to take charge of situations and influence their outcome. Once we have the sense of being in charge of things, we feel—and are—more powerful.

Effective listening can reduce stress and tension; for example, giving others a chance to share their problems may clear the air. Take a case where you are one of the problems. Allowing that person to vent negative feelings toward you alleviates the feeling. You can then progress with the communication. The following is an example of allowing someone to vent their negative feelings that led to a positive outcome.

A manager named Steve met with a manager from a related department. "Joan," he said, "I have the feeling there's something that disturbs you about our professional relationship." Joan took this encouragement as an opportunity and explained that she felt he made some very degrading comments to her a week ago.

Instead of reacting defensively, Steve listened to Joan's whole story and acknowledged her feelings. "I appreciate your telling me," he said. "I can see how you thought my comments were a putdown."

"Yes," Joan remarked, "I was upset about it."

Steve listened to that, too, and expressed concern that Joan was upset, adding, "I didn't intend it as a putdown."

This listening encounter proved a success. A few days later, Joan was heard mentioning her rapport with Steve as an example of a good working relationship.

Imagine what might have happened if Steve had reacted defensively to Joan after inviting her to discuss what was bothering her! Often, when we offer someone the opportunity to express his or her feelings about our behavior, we feel attacked and find it difficult to handle the feedback as Steve did. Usually we take what is being said personally and become defensive.

If Steve had responded defensively to Joan's expressed feelings, the conversation more than likely would have ended with no resolution and possibly increased negative feelings. Defensive listening is a major barrier to efficient communication and problem solving because it perpetuates nonlistening and an argumentative atmosphere.

Conversely, true listening promotes cooperation; it assumes the other person has worth, dignity, and something to offer. This attitude makes the other person feel positive. People who feel you are honestly interested in them and value their thoughts and opinions will more readily see your point of view. They will take a more positive attitude toward being with you and working with you.

Listening to others gives us the information needed to make the most of our communication. Listening to *ourselves* gives us the information to act in our own best interests. As we achieve self-awareness, we are more able to choose our responses rather than react automatically. We respond to what is real, rather than emotions or misconceptions.

Information is power. Effective listeners are able to concentrate and find the most valid information in whatever they hear. Effective listeners are powerful people.

It takes a certain amount of time and effort to learn to listen effectively, but in the long run it saves time. We don't have to go back and correct mistakes or clean up misunderstood communications. We meet our needs and those of others more quickly.

PRACTICE SESSION

As a way to increase your listening awareness, list all the sounds you hear in the next five minutes. Do this two to three times a day in different environments to sharpen your listening awareness and skill.

Doing this will increase your listening awareness. It will help you realize how sharp your listening can become when you take the time to listen specifically to the sounds around you. People often become aware of how different environments influence how well they listen. They discover how much of their time is spent in passive hearing rather than effective listening.

LEVELS OF LISTENING

Listening can be divided into three levels, characterized by certain behaviors that affect listening efficiency. These levels are not sharply distinct, but general categories into which people fall; they may overlap or interchange depending on what is happening. As we move from level 3 to level 1, our potential for understanding, retention, and effective communication increases. All of us listen at different levels of efficiency throughout the day, depending on the circumstances and the people involved. For instance, most often people have difficulty listening effectively when in a conflict situation, when dealing with emotional people, when criticism is being directed at them, when they are being disciplined, or when feeling anxious, fearful, or angry. Others listen effectively on the job but tune out when they get home.

The following descriptions of the three levels will help you understand the ways you listen.

Three Levels of Listening

Level 1:   Empathetic listening. At this level, listeners refrain from judging the talker and place themselves in the other's position, attempting to see things from his or her point of view. Some characteristics of this level include being aware and in the present moment; acknowledging and responding; not letting oneself be distracted; paying attention to the speaker's total communication, including body language; being empathetic to the speaker's feelings and thoughts; and suspending one's own thoughts and feeling to give attention solely to listening. Empathetic listening requires an OK–OK attitude. It also requires that the listener show both verbally and nonverbally that he or she is truly listening. The overall focus is to listen from the heart, which opens the doorway to understanding, caring, and empathy.

Level 2:   Hearing words, but not really listening. At this level, people stay at the surface of the communication and do not understand the deeper meanings of what is being said. They try to hear what the speaker is saying but make little effort to understand the speaker's intent. Level 2 listeners tend to listen logically, being concerned about content more than feeling, and remain emotionally detached from the conversation. Level 2 listening can lead to dangerous misunderstandings because the listener is concentrating only slightly on what is said. At level 3 it is obvious that the person is not listening; however, at level 2 the speaker may be lulled into a false sense of being listened to and understood.

Level 3:   Listening in spurts. Tuning in and tuning out, being somewhat aware of others, but mainly paying attention to oneself. One follows the discussion only enough to get a chance to talk. Level 3 listening is quiet, passive listening without responding. Often a person listening at this level is faking attention while thinking about unrelated matters, making judgments, forming rebuttals or advice, or preparing what he or she wants to say next. The listener may display a blank stare and is more interested in talking than listening.

Most of us listen at all three levels during the course of a day. However, the goal is to listen at level 1 in all situations.

EXERCISE 1.2	Think for a moment about your day.

1. How often did you listen at level 1?

    (a)   When?

    (b)   With whom?

2. What is your characteristic listening approach?

    (a) A combination of the three levels?

    (b) Emphasis on one in particular? Which one?

Growth begins with awareness. By paying attention to your listening style, you can start this awareness process, a process that can result in improved communication and relationships.

LISTENING ASSESSMENT EXERCISE

To help you start to be more aware of your listening habits, complete the following listening self-evaluation. It will give you an idea of which listening habits you can be happy about and which ones you might want to reshape. Answer each question thoughtfully.

EFFECTIVE COMMUNICATING SELF-EVALUATION

Communicating Knowledge and Attitudes	Most of the Time	Frequently	Occasionally	Almost Never
Put an X in the appropriate column.				
Do you:				
1. Tune out people who say something you don't agree with or don't want to hear?	_____	_____	_____	_____
2. Concentrate on what is being said even if you are not really interested?	_____	_____	_____	_____

Communicating Knowledge and Attitudes	Most of the Time	Frequently	Occasionally	Almost Never
3. Assume you know what the talker is going to say and stop listening?	_____	_____	_____	_____
4. Repeat in your own words what the talker has just said?	_____	_____	_____	_____
5. Listen to the other person's viewpoint, even if it differs from yours?	_____	_____	_____	_____
6. Learn something from each person you meet, even if it is ever so slight?	_____	_____	_____	_____
7. Find out what words mean when they are used in ways not familiar to you?	_____	_____	_____	_____
8. Form a rebuttal in your head while the speaker is talking?	_____	_____	_____	_____
9. Give the appearance of listening when you aren't?	_____	_____	_____	_____
10. Daydream while the speaker is talking?	_____	_____	_____	_____
11. Listen to the whole message—what the talker is saying verbally and nonverbally?	_____	_____	_____	_____
12. Recognize that words don't mean exactly the same thing to different people?	_____	_____	_____	_____
13. Listen to only what you want to hear, blotting out the talker's whole message?	_____	_____	_____	_____
14. Look at the person who is talking?	_____	_____	_____	_____
15. Concentrate on the talker's meaning rather than how he or she looks?	_____	_____	_____	_____
16. Know which words and phrases you respond to emotionally?	_____	_____	_____	_____
17. Think about what you want to accomplish with your communication?	_____	_____	_____	_____
18. Plan the best time to say what you want to say?	_____	_____	_____	_____
19. Think about how the other person might react to what you say?	_____	_____	_____	_____
20. Consider the best way to make your communication (written, spoken, phone, bulletin board, memo, etc.) work?	_____	_____	_____	_____
21. Think about what kind of person you're talking to (worried, hostile, disinterested, rushed, shy, stubborn, impatient, etc.)?	_____	_____	_____	_____
22. Interrupt the talker while he or she is still talking?	_____	_____	_____	_____
23. Think, "I assumed he or she would know that"?	_____	_____	_____	_____

Communicating Knowledge and Attitudes	Most of the Time	Frequently	Occasionally	Almost Never
24. Allow the talker to vent negative feelings toward you without becoming defensive?	_____	_____	_____	_____
25. Practice regularly to increase your listening efficiency?	_____	_____	_____	_____
26. Take notes when necessary to help you to remember?	_____	_____	_____	_____
27. Hear noises without being distracted by them?	_____	_____	_____	_____
28. Listen to the talker without judging or criticizing?	_____	_____	_____	_____
29. Restate instructions and messages to be sure you understand correctly?	_____	_____	_____	_____
30. Paraphrase what you believe the talker is feeling?	_____	_____	_____	_____

Scoring Index

Circle the number that matches the time frame (most of the time, frequently, etc.) you checked on each of the 30 items of the self-evaluation.

Example: *If you put a ✓ under "frequently" for number 1, you would circle 2 in the "frequently" column.*

Then, add the circled scores in each of the columns. Now, write the scores of each column in the lines under each time frame category.

	Most of the Time	Frequently	Occasionally	Almost Never
1.	1	2	3	4
2.	4	3	2	1
3.	1	2	3	4
4.	4	3	2	1
5.	4	3	2	1
6.	4	3	2	1
7.	4	3	2	1
8.	1	2	3	4
9.	1	2	3	4
10.	1	2	3	4

(continued)

	Most of the Time	Frequently	Occasionally	Almost Never
11.	4	3	2	1
12.	4	3	2	1
13.	1	2	3	4
14.	4	3	2	1
15.	4	3	2	1
16.	4	3	2	1
17.	4	3	2	1
18.	4	3	2	1
19.	4	3	2	1
20.	4	3	2	1
21.	4	3	2	1
22.	1	2	3	4
23.	1	2	3	4
24.	4	3	2	1
25.	4	3	2	1
26.	4	3	2	1
27.	4	3	2	1
28.	4	3	2	1
29.	4	3	2	1
30.	4	3	2	1
Totals	_____	_____	_____	_____

Total of items circled in each column:

Most of the Time		Frequently		Occasionally		Almost Never		Total
_____	+	_____	+	_____	+	_____	=	_____

Scoring: 110–120 Superior   _____
          99–109   Above Average   _____
          88–98   Average   _____
          77–87   Fair   _____

Action Plan: Reexamine your responses. What questions do you feel you want to modify and/or improve upon? Pick three to start working on. To get you started on modifying your behavior, complete the following affirmation exercise.

EXERCISE 1.3

Develop an affirmation for each category. This exercise will help you modify and improve the behaviors you listed.

In listening, what I want to accomplish is:

In work, what I want to accomplish through listening is:

In my personal life, what I want to accomplish through listening is:

Here is a short, anonymous article someone sent me in the mail:

Could You Just Listen?[3]

When I ask you to listen to me and you start giving me advice, you have not done what I asked. When I ask you to listen to me and you begin to tell me why I shouldn't feel that way, you are trampling on my feelings. When I ask you to listen to me and you feel you have to do something to solve my problem, you have failed me—strange as that may seem.

Listen! All I ask is that you *listen,* not talk or do, just hear me. Advice is cheap. Fifty cents will give you both Dear Abby and Billy Graham in the same paper.

When you do something for me that I can and need to do for myself, you contribute to my fear and inadequacy, but when you accept as a simple fact that I do feel what I feel no matter how irrational, then I can quit trying to convince you and get down to the business of understanding it.

Irrational feelings make sense when we understand what's behind them, and when that's clear, the answers are obvious and I don't need advice. Perhaps that's why prayer works sometimes for some people—because God is mute and doesn't give advice to try to fix things. God just listens and lets you work it out for yourself.

So please just listen. If you want to talk, wait a minute for your turn and I'll listen to you.

SELF-TEST   To evaluate how well you have learned the information on this chapter, see how many of the questions you can answer without reviewing the chapter material.

1. What percentage of time do people generally spend in the four modes of communicating?

   writing _____%

   reading _____%

   speaking _____%

   listening _____%

2. What is the average listening efficiency? _____%

3. What are the three levels of listening? List them and write a sentence or two describing each level.

4. List three advantages of learning to listen effectively.

ANSWERS

1. Writing 9%, reading 16%, talking 35%, listening 40%

2. 25%

3. Level 1   Listening nonjudgmentally with understanding to the intent and feelings, paying attention to the speaker's total communication, processing what is being said

   Level 2   Hearing words but not making an effort to understand the speaker's intent, appearing to listen intently when in fact only slightly concentrating

   Level 3   Listening in spurts, more hearing going on than listening; being passive, judgmental

4. Advantages to listening effectively:

• Improved supervisory skills when dealing with employees who have a problem

• Decreased time spent in solving problems

• Improved self-esteem and self-confidence because you relate more effectively with others

• Increased productivity, more information remembered, and decreased misunderstanding

• Fewer mistakes made because you listened to the instructions

• Increased respect, trust, and rapport with co-workers

2 How You Got to Be the Listener You Are

One friend, one person who is truly understanding, who takes the trouble to listen to us as we consider our problem, can change our whole outlook on the world.

Dr. Elton Mayo

The Effective Communicating Self-Evaluation in Chapter 1 provided you with some insight into your listening style and habits. Awareness is the first step in modifying and improving our behavior.

If you are beginning to realize that your listening skill could use some work, you are normal. Considering how important listening is to our human relationships, our personal development, and our effective working transactions, it can be embarrassing to realize how ineffective we are at it. It almost seems that humans are not listening-oriented beings.

FROM CRADLE TO CHILDHOOD TO ADULTHOOD

We lack skill as listeners for many reasons, some personal, some more or less universal. They have to do with childhood experiences, formal training, psychological limitations, and socialized attitudes.

Our attitudes toward listening begin in the crib. A baby who is just lying there, doing the infant equivalent of listening, gets no attention. However, the minute the baby begins to cry, the infant equivalent of speaking up, Mommy or Daddy usually comes and picks the baby up, speaks, or pays some other kind of attention. Any attention is what the baby craves. Even negative attention ("Stop that crying!") is better than no attention at all. The message the infant receives is that talking earns more rewards than listening—a message repeated over and over during infancy.

As the child grows older, the parents and other significant people in the child's life communicate additional messages about listening. Sometimes these messages are verbal; sometimes they are nonverbal. Following are some of the influential verbal messages many people receive as children:

"Don't argue with me."
"You don't know what you're talking about."
"Don't interrupt your elders."
"Don't be forward."
"Shut up and listen."
"Children should be seen and not heard."
"Be quiet."
"You're too young to understand."
"Don't speak until you're spoken to."
"Look at me when I shout at you."

EXERCISE 2.1

You might want to put a check by the messages above that you received as a child. By examining the ramifications of these messages in your present behavior, you might be surprised to find out how your past experiences are influencing your present listening habits.

How have the messages you checked influenced your current listening behavior? Use the space below to write down your examples.

EXERCISE 2.1
(continued)

These additional questions will help you explore in more detail how your past might still be affecting your behavior.

Do you avoid presenting an alternative view of an issue, so as not to argue with the talker?   Yes _____.   No _____.   If yes, with whom?

What could you do to start offering your point of view?

Who might assist you in developing your ability to share your ideas?

Does your listening behavior change when you are talking to a person of greater authority?   Yes _____.   No _____.   If yes, how does it change and with whom?

What could you do to modify this behavior?

Do you experience a similar behavior when you are talking to people older than you?   Yes _____.   No. _____.   If yes, with whom? When?

What could you do to modify this behavior?

At first glance, some of the negative messages might seem to be encouragements to listen. However, as you were examining them and their ramifications, you probably began to experience some discomfort. A child who hears these messages also feels discomfort, and this discomfort seems to be associated with listening. The messages may even plant seeds of resistance to listening in the child's mind. For example, a child who repeatedly hears someone say, "Shut up and listen!" may think consciously or unconsciously, "I will not shut up and listen and no one is going to make me." There is a strong possibility that this child will grow up to be a poor listener.

EXERCISE 2.2

What positive statements could replace the negative one mentioned above? List as many as you can. I'll get you started.

- I'll listen to what you have to say after I'm finished.

- I feel good when you listen to me.

STROKES

One factor influencing how people get to be the listeners they are is how they were stroked as children. How children are listened to can be negative or positive strokes. A child's behavior is often formed by the way he or she is paid attention to or receives recognition from others, a phenomenon dealt with by the late Dr. Eric Berne, author of *Games People Play*. Through his research, Dr. Berne found that strokes were a vital aspect in the formulation of behavioral patterns. Every person has a need to be touched and recognized by others. A stroke is any form of recognition or attention one person gives to another. Strokes can be positive or negative. They can be given in the form of physical touching or nonverbal behaviors such as looks, winks, frowns, smiles, or gestures. Verbal strokes could be compliments or criticisms. Strokes are a survival need. Often, negative strokes are sent to children, and the parents don't realize the impact they have on a child's self-concept.

People often relate the following examples of how they were stroked negatively:

"I was told angrily to shut up."
"I got negative strokes for speaking up."
"I certainly couldn't disagree, and if I did I sure heard about it."
"If I didn't listen, I would get a spanking."

One person said she got negative strokes for interrupting. She complied to the letter, but was left feeling that her ideas weren't as important as others. Her brother, on the other hand, rebelled against the message and interrupted often, whereupon he was spanked or sent to his room. As an adult, this behavior pattern resulted in his being seen as insubordinate and not of management potential.

Mary provides an example that most people can relate to:

I couldn't understand why listening was so painful to me until one day during a heated discussion with a co-worker . . . the light bulb went on. I had asked this co-worker quietly several times to bring me a report I needed. When she didn't bring it to me, I raised my voice and told her to bring it to me "right now." This resulted in an angry discussion during which the co-worker said, "I know I don't have to listen to you the first couple of times because you always repeat what you're saying to me."

That's when the light bulb went on. She was right; I do repeat over and over again what I want from others and end up saying it angrily. And you know . . . that is exactly what my parents did to me. I guess listening became painful because it often ended with someone angrily yelling at me. And here I'm doing the same thing to others!

Listening is one of the finest strokes one person can give another. When people have been listened to, they leave the encounter feeling that what they have said has been heard. When people don't feel they have been "tuned out" and have been listened to nonjudgmentally and non-critically, they see themselves as worthy of attention. This kind of listening has a positive effect on the talker's self-esteem. Level 1 listening is a way to have a positive influence on others, because it comes from the heart's intelligence.

For instance, when a secretary suddenly begins to make a number of typing errors, mumbles under her breath, and snaps at a co-worker, a boss who is paying attention may say something like, "You seem upset about something. Can I help?" To be listened to can make one feel understood and worthwhile as a human being. On the other hand, if the boss had been critical ("You shouldn't lose your temper and snap at people!"), the secretary, who is already feeling out of sorts, would take his critical comment as a real putdown and her feelings would more than likely accelerate.

We can also stroke others by how we listen to them nonverbally. Often, a listener turns a talker off by a certain look, a shift in body posture to a closed position, or an impatient tapping of fingers on a desk or table. When we listen with an attentive look, lean forward with interest, or have an open body posture, we nonverbally stroke the talker in a positive way.

To help you be more aware of various nonverbal actions that can have a negative and/or positive impact on people, complete the following exercise.

EXERCISE 2.3

Take a few minutes to think of the many nonverbal ways that other people let you know they are listening to you, and that are felt, seen, or heard as positive and negative strokes.

	Nonverbal Positive Strokes	*Nonverbal Negative Strokes*

Facial expression:

Body posture:

EXERCISE 2.3
(continued)

Gestures:

Tone of voice:

Other:

SOCIALIZATION PROCESS

All children live in a social environment that influences the type of behavior patterns they develop. As children's spheres of experience grow, they incorporate into their own personalities those of the people close to them—parents, grandparents, older siblings, teachers, and so on—who interact with them every day over a long time period. The effects have several dimensions.

The way in which adults listen to children tells children something about themselves. Parents who interrupt their children, look stern while listening, ignore their children's feelings, or turn away when their children are talking send a message that what the children have to say is stupid or unimportant. This has a negative effect on the children's self-concept—an effect that lasts well into adulthood. As a result, listening ability is hampered. Studies show that when people are anxious or worried about approval, they have trouble concentrating on what is being said.

Margaret's father looked at her disapprovingly when she talked to him about ideas that he didn't agree with. He would often interrupt her in the middle of a sentence to tell her she was wrong. As a result of the childhood experience, she had difficulty concentrating when anyone in authority talked to her. She would concentrate on how she was coming across to the other person, not on what the person was saying.

Adults' listening behaviors serve as models for the child's behavior. Children do what they see adults (particularly their parents) do. Children are excellent mimics, and it takes them practically no time at all to learn listening behavior from their adult models. If parents constantly talk *at* each other and do not respond to each other's feelings, if they communicate their judgmental attitudes through their posture or facial expression, or if they give each other and their children little acknowledgment, the children will mimic their behavior.

My father used to frown when concentrating on something. I thought he was angry or upset with me until I later found out that he was only concentrating on what I was saying. I certainly experienced some anxiety until I found this out. When I started conducting seminars, I discovered that *I* frowned a lot while concentrating on what the talker was saying, and attendees thought I was being critical of them. It took an awareness of this facial expression and a great deal of effort to stop a behavior learned from my father that was causing problems in my professional life.

A young man reported a more severe problem than mine; he had great trouble listening to people.

John constantly tuned others out while they were talking and he couldn't seem to break this habit. It upset him because he was having trouble at work listening to directions and paying attention during meetings. As it happened, his mother had been a nonstop talker who ignored his needs. To keep his own sanity, he had learned to shut her out of his consciousness. He became so good at tuning her out that he generalized this behavior—ultimately tuning other people out as well. It took a lot of work to overcome this deeply ingrained response.

People tend to duplicate, throughout their lives, the relationship patterns they experienced in their early years. This means that if we were not listened to as children, we will be likely, as adults, to find other people who don't listen to us. We may also have a tendency to be nonlisteners. We will then become even more uncomfortable in nonlistening situations and will find it increasingly difficult to listen actively and responsively. Once a pattern takes hold, it can be difficult to break.

A manager became aware of his nonlistening habit while participating in a listening exercise. I had noticed early in the seminar that he was probably listening at level 3 or 2. When I asked for a show of hands from those who thought they were level 1 listeners, he was among those who raised their hands. However, when he had to summarize what the other person said during a listening exercise, he discovered he couldn't.

When I suggested that this might be a learned behavior from his childhood, he quickly discounted my suggestion. The next morning, he confided to me that he had thought about what I had said and that I had been right. His parents had often ignored him and were busy doing other things when he talked to them. He remembered how frustrated and unloved he felt. He went on to say that his family told him he didn't listen to them, but he denied it and disbelieved them, too. He was grateful that he had the opportunity to discover his true, nonlistening habit.

This socialization process is a determining factor in people's development of certain listening patterns. Being aware of this process and how it influences listening styles can help us overcome patterns that result in dissatisfaction and frustration.

EXERCISE 2.4

Take a few minutes to examine the following questions about your socialization process. Completing this profile will let you uncover elements that may have affected your present listening patterns.

The Family System

1. How did your parents listen to you when you were young?

    _____ With complete attention.

    _____ Asked so many questions I thought I was being interrogated.

    _____ With divided attention.

    _____ Reluctantly.

    _____ Showed little interest.

    _____ Interrupted me.

    _____ Did something else while saying, "Hmmm," "Uh-huh."

    _____ Other.

How did you respond to this kind of attention?

What did you say to yourself?

How do you think this kind of attention has affected your present listening habits?

2. The communication with my parents was:

_____ indirect   _____ direct

_____ not really honest   _____ honest

_____ vague   _____ clear   _____ specific

_____ open   _____ closed

_____ pleasant   _____ unpleasant   _____ painful

_____ relaxed   _____ stressful   _____ up-tight

_____ double messages were sent

_____ what was said was meant

_____other

3. The rules in my family were:

_____ flexible   _____ rigid   _____ formal

_____ human   _____ inhuman

_____ nonnegotiable   _____ negotiable

_____ closed   _____ open   _____ binding

_____ clearly defined   _____ uncertain

_____ hazy   _____ understood

_____ appropriate   _____ redefinable

_____ changeable   _____ unchangeable

EXERCISE 2.4
(continued)

Were you allowed to be part of making the rules and setting your own limitations? _____ Yes _____ No

How does this family system affect you as an adult listener and communicator?

How does it affect you on the job?

OK Attitudes

The socialization process includes the attitude of "OKness" in relation to self and others. According to Dr. Berne's theory, there are four attitudes (1) I'm OK–You're OK, (2) I'm OK–You're Not OK, (3) I'm Not OK–You're OK, and (4) I'm Not OK–You're Not OK either, so there!

The listening behavior of individuals in the different OK attitudes varies; thus, each has different listening characteristics that include one's beliefs about oneself and others, beliefs that in turn influence the attitudes and ways a person interacts with others.

Greg's father's style of listening matched the "I'm OK–You're Not OK" pattern. Greg, a supervisor in a large federal agency, incorporated many of his father's listening behaviors. As a result, his employees didn't feel that he listened to them. Greg had the attitude, "Who needs to bother listening to 'Not OK' people; they don't have good ideas anyway."

Others in the office often complained that Greg listened to them with a critical expression on his face. He would quickly judge and criticize what they had said, and he seemed to listen only to what he had to say, as if he were the only one who had good ideas. When someone brought up an opposing point of view, Greg would hear what he wanted to hear, filtering out comments he didn't agree with. His manner and listening style often left people feeling frustrated and resentful. Thus, Greg listened much the same way as his father, not realizing how his behavior was negatively affecting others. In other words, this listening behavior was in his blind area—he wasn't aware of it but others were.

Maria, on the other hand, held the "I'm Not OK–You're OK" attitude. Her behavior was very different from Greg's. She often worried about herself and how she was coming across. She focused on herself rather than on the dynamics of what was going on between herself and others. She was so busy trying to say the right thing that she usually didn't say anything. During meetings, she was reluctant to speak up because she believed what she had to say would be stupid. She often said, "I will probably say something dumb, so why bother!" Because she was behaving from the "Not OK" attitude, she usually listened at level 2 or 3. The consequences were instructions carried out poorly, messages taken down incorrectly, and frequent criticism from her supervisor.

The "Not OK–Not OK" position is very detrimental to listening and the entire communication process. People behaving from this position vacillate between the two OK attitudes mentioned earlier. They listen most often from level 3 and, as a result, do not hear others. They do not make the effort to listen to what others say. Since neither they nor the others are OK, they find very little reason to bother listening and are rarely interested in what anyone has to say. They are usually perceived as uninterested in others, withdrawn, negative, and pessimistic. This behavior leads nowhere. It's felt by those experiencing it as "going around in circles," ending in frustration, anger, and discouragement. You'll hear these people say, "I can't do anything; there's nothing anyone can do!" Because of the attitude, not much *does* get done. Problems don't get resolved, and the same ones crop up over and over.

On the other hand, if parents, teachers, and other adults model effective listening behavior by focusing attention on talkers, acknowledging speakers without being judgmental, and communicating through their faces, bodies, tones of voice, and words that the talkers are important, children will be more likely to develop positive concepts, exhibit effective listening behavior, and operate from the "OK–OK" attitude. Effective listening patterns, as well as nonlistening patterns, can become habitual. Undesirable patterns *can* be changed, although it requires continual awareness and practice.

Where the "Not OK" styles usually close off communication, "OK–OK" style is categorized as open, relaxed, understanding, logical, empathetic, and nonjudgmental.

Lee described his parents as understanding and easy to talk to, tolerant, and accepting of his behavior. Whenever he had a problem, they would listen from their hearts and help him come to a solution while supporting his decision and encouraging him to follow it through.

As a manager, he applied these same listening skills to the people on the job. His expectations of himself and others were realistic and valid. People felt comfortable around him because he didn't quickly judge or criticize. He had a mutual respect for himself and others while accepting the significance of people. Co-workers often said, "I like him; he really listens to me."

Like Janet in Chapter 1, he listened with understanding, had an open mind, and didn't interrupt or ask unnecessary questions. He often reflected feelings that were expressed by paraphrasing for understanding and summarizing for mutual clarification.

Being aware of this "OK" phenomenon, this aspect of human behavior and how it influences listening, can be beneficial in quickly improving listening behaviors. It's an easy way to modify your behavior in a short time.

Drama Triangle

Another aspect of the socialization process is the "drama triangle." When individuals act from the "Not OK" behavior mode, they frequently participate in a drama triangle that has three types of participants: persecutor, rescuer, and victim.[4]

The *persecutor* operates from the "I'm OK–You're Not OK" position. People behaving in this mode often are fault-finding and nit-picking, can't wait to say "gotcha," and are blemish players; no matter what you pass over their desk, they find something wrong with it and might even circle the mistake in red to make sure you have to do it over again. Persecutors are experts at zeroing in on what people do that's wrong, rather than right. Their management and supervisory styles are to "manage by exception—what goes wrong is what is paid attention to." If something is out of line, they give a negative stroke. They are quick to form a rebuttal to what has been said and often listen to how something is going to fail or nor work. People often feel as if they are being treated like dumb and stupid children after communicating with a persecutor. One of the participants in a listening seminar I conducted had this example of a manager that dealt with him and his co-workers from the persecutor mode.

I can't think of a time when this manager would express any kind of appreciation for the good work my co-workers and I did. He would say we should do good work because we were getting paid for doing it, but he never missed a chance to criticize us when our work wasn't perfect. If anyone of us made a mistake his reaction was like a death penalty. Am I ever glad I don't work for him anymore. There isn't anyone I worked with that is still there. They've all left.

Rescuers are advice givers. They take onto their backs other people's monkeys and make the problems their own. These people are rescuing others who don't need to be rescued, don't want to be rescued, or aren't asking to be rescued—but they rescue them anyway because it's good for them! They take on others' responsibility, when it would be better if others were responsible for themselves. Like persecutors, they are operating from the "I'm OK–You're Not OK" attitude. They have a strong need to be needed. They tell their employees what they should do, and when it doesn't go right they get blamed and thus end up as victims.

Rescuers tend to be lousy delegators—"gotta do it themselves." This results in feeling victimized because their own work doesn't get done and pressures build up. They end up working 10 to 12 hours when everyone else is going home on time.

This overcare behavior leads to dependency relationships between themselves and others. It interferes with other people learning to solve their own problems, doing their own thinking, and figuring out for themselves what would be the best choice to make. They become indispensable and have constant interruptions during the day. When a person is talking, rescuers are so busy thinking of the best advice to give that they don't listen to the whole problem; as a result, the advice given is often inappropriate.

Tim, a supervisor, found out that he often listened and behaved from the rescuer mode. He decided that not only was it detrimental to his employees' professional growth, it also left him little time for his own work, and he was plagued by interruptions. He found some distinct advantages to giving it up: He had more time for himself, he finished his own projects on time (resulting in less hassle from his boss), he felt decreased stress and tension, and the people he supervised became more self-reliant and confident. He said he had to be on his toes to stop himself from giving advice, often stopping himself in the middle of a sentence. Tim discovered that his listening habits changed. Because he stopped forming advice in his head while the person was talking, he listened more frequently at level 1. As a consequence, he remembered more of what was said to him.

Like Tim, some people behave from the rescuer mode by taking on others' responsibilities and doing others' work, thus not having time to do their own. When people do this, they end up victims. Therefore, they have moved from the rescuer mode to the victim mode. Others *start* in the victim mode by behaving in such a way that they incite others to "kick" them verbally, nonverbally, emotionally, or physically.

When people start out in the victim mode, they are operating from the "I'm Not OK–You're OK" attitude in ways that result in their getting negative strokes: not listening to directions, allowing their emotions to override their objectivity, and becoming defensive instead of listening. Marie, a secretary in a computer company, discovered she behaved from this position in her relationship with others—especially her boss:

> I often feel like a victim in my interactions with my boss. I think he is the persecutor and I'm the victim. For example, late Thursday afternoon, my boss gave me a 20-page project with graphs and numerical tables to type and finish by Monday at 10 a.m. I didn't listen to the time he stated when he handed me the project. Instead, I was busy figuring out how I was going to get it done and finish the other work I had on my desk. All I heard was Monday.
>
> As I look back on this situation, I can see that by not being clear on the time, I was already setting myself up to be a victim. Discussing with him my concern about getting it out on Monday, along with completing the other assignments on my desk, would have kept me out of the victim position.
>
> In any event, I didn't take either of these options. Instead, I became nervous and frustrated, which led to errors and my typing the project more slowly. By 10 a.m. Monday morning, I had it typed but not proofread. You can imagine my surprise when my boss asked for it! I told him I didn't hear him say it was due at 10 a.m. It was finished, but not proofread. Naturally, he became angry at my comment that I didn't hear him say it was due at 10 a.m. and he said a few choice words I won't repeat. However, he reluctantly extended the time by an hour so I could get it proofread.

Well, by this time I was so nervous I had to have a cup of coffee. I took the report down to the cafeteria. Again, I can see this was another set-up on my part to end up victim. You don't take important projects to the cafeteria. It would have been better to forgo the coffee until after I'd proofread the material, but . . . I didn't!

While I was proofreading, an emergency came up. In my hurry to take care of the emergency, I left the report on the table, completely forgetting it. Guess who came down to the cafeteria and found the report? Yep! My boss. He brought the report to me and said critically, "Are you by any chance looking for this?" and threw it on my desk. Was I embarrassed!

This example was just one of the many ways Marie discovered that she set herself up to be victim. Upon examining her listening habits, she found that her nonlistening habits resulted in other kinds of nonproductive behavior such as not completing tasks as directed. She discovered she talked to herself mentally while her boss was giving her instructions. This internal dialogue distracted her from what was being said. She found she could stop this internal process by being aware of it, stopping the dialogue, and then summarizing what the other person said as a way of checking her listening.

These "OK" attitudes play a major part in each person's listening behavior. As you can see from the graph that follows, these attitudes of "OKness" are formed early in childhood. They are a reflection of our self-concept, and they influence attitudes about others that can result in ineffective or effective listening behavior. Being aware of what "OK" attitudes we are listening from can be a giant step in improving our listening habits.

This socialization process is an important ingredient in determining the "OK" attitudes from which people behave. It is a significant factor that causes many of the listening problems people experience. Graphically, the process is summarized in Figure 2.1.

School

There are few rewards for listening—mainly punishments for not listening. This situation carries over into school. We are rewarded when we do well at reading, speaking, and writing, but listening skill wins little direct praise. Although we get a high grade when we have listened enough in class to do well on a test, no one specifically connects this

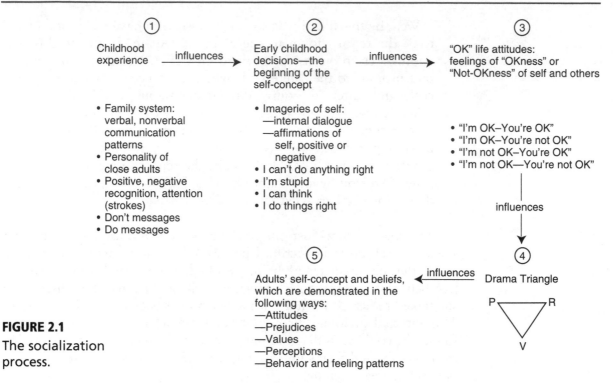

FIGURE 2.1

The socialization process.

grade to listening. A person who gets an A is said to have "learned" the material, but not to have "listened well." Few report cards comment on listening improvement. Yet, if we give inappropriate responses in class sessions or on a test, we may very well be accused of not having listened. Listening is the channel most often used for learning—more than reading, writing, or speaking.

In addition, our formal training in communication is backwards. Figure 2.2 shows the amount of training we get in each of the communication modes, compared to the percentage of time we use that type of communication.

Apparently, the school system has accepted the myth that we were born knowing how to listen. Only recently are courses in listening being offered, and these are mostly for adults. Most of us seldom get any training or practice in active listening during our developmental years. However, in recent years there has been a movement within the school system to include some listening activities as part of the basic school curriculum. By teaching children caring heart-listening the teachers help the children activate their heart-knowing capabilities. Imagine how this

FIGURE 2.2

Years of training versus time used for each mode of communication.

Mode of Communication	Formal Years Training	Percentage of Time Used
Writing	12 years	9%
Reading	6–8 years	16%
Speaking	1–2 years	35%
Listening	0–$\frac{1}{2}$ years	40%

heart-listening training could influence these children and their relationships with their families and friends.

Of course, all the active, responsible adult listeners in a person's life may have trouble counteracting the effects of one significant childhood influence: television. Many recent studies indicate that heavy TV-watching encourages passivity and can stunt the growth of the imagination. At the very least, it discourages the active listening habit. Unfortunately, if we have been members of the TV generation, we are already influenced to some extent.

Listening through Filters

We are often unaware of how our childhood experiences influence our adult behavior. The socialization process results in our listening through filters. Our brain processes each new piece of experience through filters that have various forms. Figure 2.3 shows some of the filters that exert the greatest influence.

Although these filters are within us, we are often blind to them. It is important to develop the ability to become conscious of these blind

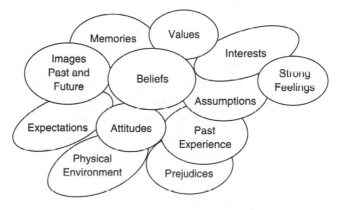

FIGURE 2.3

Filters that affect how we listen.

spots that often result in unproductive behavior. We will then have an opportunity to understand and reshape our beliefs, values, and attitudes.

Because people aren't aware of their beliefs, they have little opportunity to understand them and/or reshape them. When people aren't aware of how their beliefs influence what they value about work and their attitude toward certain behaviors in others, they find it difficult to listen to other people's points of view or accept their behavior.

Say, for instance, I'm your supervisor, and I strongly believe that when people talk and enjoy their work they aren't getting their work done properly. Because of my belief, I value silence and seriousness on the job. I also have the attitude that people who kid around don't perform as they "should" and are more trouble than they are worth.

On the other hand, you believe that a relaxed and enjoyable working environment keeps work from being drudgery and makes it acceptable. Because of this belief, you value an understanding, easygoing supervisor. You have the attitude that a supervisor who doesn't kid around a little is a "turkey."

Now, if we both are unaware of our attitudes, we would probably have difficulty dealing with each other. We would both find it arduous listening to the other's point of view, since the views are in opposition. Our beliefs could even lead to contempt for each other, thus interfering with our ability to work things out.

The belief that we hold in reference to each other's work behavior will result in both of us having certain expectations of each other, and because our beliefs are so different, our expectations are rarely realized, leaving us both disappointed and frustrated. On the other hand, if both of us could gain understanding of our own as well as the other's belief, we might start listening to each other's point of view and be able to listen to each other from the heart without judgment.

Self-Knowledge

Self-knowledge is an import ingredient for increasing the ability to communicate and interact effectively with others. The following analogy, illustrated by Figure 2.4, is one way to look at the self-knowledge process.

If you look at a globe as you stand in front of it, you can see part of it. If you divide the part you can see in half, one half represents the parts of ourselves we are conscious of. These are aspects of our listening

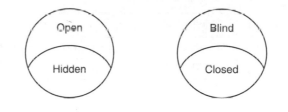

FIGURE 2.4

Analogy of the self-knowledge process.

behavior we can identify and recognize. Since we are open to these behaviors and they are useful, we can pat ourselves on the back and say, "A job well done!" On the other hand, if we don't like them and the results aren't what we want, we can reshape them.

The other half of the globe is the portion of ourselves we keep hidden. For instance, some people keep a worthy idea hidden from their managers because the managers might steal their ideas and take the credit for them. Other people keep their feelings hidden because they have been belittled. One woman said, "I've stopped talking about how I feel about things to my boss because I was told, 'You shouldn't feel that way,' and 'Don't make mountains out of molehills.'"

The portions of the globe you cannot see are the blind and closed areas. The blind area hides sides of ourselves that we took a peek at and didn't like, therefore fooling us into thinking that the behavior wasn't really important enough to change. It can also include our characteristics that we don't like. Consequently, we project the same qualities onto others that we deny in ourselves. Others know about these characteristics and would be happy to tell us about them if we asked. For one reason or another, we are blind to certain sides of ourselves, and our behavior often gets us into trouble in our relationships with others.

The closed area is one we have shut off from ourselves because we have found it too distasteful, painful, or scary. As a result, we haven't taken time to look at or explore it because of fear, lack of opportunity, or worry that we won't like what we find.[5]

Being able to identify the behavior mode you act from when you interact with individuals at work is a big step in being more effective. This type of analysis often results in broadening the open area of awareness and lessening the concealed area of consciousness. Reflection upon one's behavior is a useful tool to increase effectiveness in handling interpersonal relationships.

EXERCISE 2.5   Think of a person on the job with whom you have difficulty working.

1. Describe a recent situation that involved this person with whom you were dissatisfied.

a. What "OK" attitude were you in during this event?

b. From where in the drama triangle did you behave (persecutor, rescuer, victim)?

From where did the other person behave?

c. What seemed to start this negative situation?

d. How did it end?

e. At what level were you listening?

2. What could (will) you do in the future to modify or change this communication pattern with this person?

SUMMARY

Throughout this chapter, we talked about how our childhood experiences, the socialization process, influence how we listen as adults. As children, certain messages were expressed to us over and over again that shaped the way we formed our listening habits, habits that often result in our listening through filters of which we are not conscious.

One way to become more conscious of your listening habits and to increase your listening efficiency is to practice regularly. One useful approach is listening to difficult or unfamiliar material that challenges your mental capacities, such as attending a lecture or a program on a subject of which you have little knowledge. Effective listening does take time and effort, but it is an easy way to acquire information and ideas you can use.

Another way to increase listening efficiency is to practice listening with a planned purpose. Following are some situations you could plan in order to become aware of, evaluate, and then record your listening behavior.

- Monthly planning sessions
- Difficult customers or co-workers
- Training sessions
- Instructions
- Weekly project reviews

EXERCISE 2.6

Pick one of these each week and evaluate your listening by answering the following questions:

1. Did I listen better than I usually do?   Yes _____   No _____

   If the answer is yes, how did you listen better?

   If the answer is no, what could you do to improve your listening?

2. To become more aware of your listening habits, practice using listening checks during these situations. Whenever appropriate, summarize what you thought the talker said. Keep a record of how often you used the technique.

3. Ask for feedback from those you work with to find out if they have noticed any difference in your listening habits. Make a note of what they say you do, so that you can be more aware of this listening behavior.

SELF-TEST

As a way for you to review what you have read in this chapter, see how many of the questions you can answer without rereading the chapter.

1. At what period in one's life does listening begin?

2. Name a factor that has a strong influence on how people get to be the listeners they are.

3. Describe the behavior of someone in the "OK–OK" listening behavior mode.

4. Name the behavior modes of the drama triangle.

5. List four of the twelve filters mentioned that can influence how one listens to others.

ANSWERS

1. An infant in a crib.

2. Strokes, socialization process, family communication, patterns, usually not taught in the schools.

3. Open, understanding, logical, empathic, relaxed, nonjudgmental, uncritical, encouraging, has realistic expectations, respects others.

4. Persecutor, rescuer, victim:

   When people are behaving from the persecutor mode, they can be fault-finding and nit-picking toward themselves and others; they zero in on what is wrong and are apt to give themselves and others negative strokes. They do this by not paying attention, by being critical, and/or by being quick to form a rebuttal or give advice. When behaving from the rescuer mode, they take on other people's responsibilities, which interferes with the other person becoming self-sufficient and independent. Victims have a tendency to set themselves up to get negative strokes by not listening to directions and/or become defensive instead of listening.

5. The twelve filters mentioned are memories, images of the past and future, expectations, attitudes, the physical environment, beliefs, values, interests, strong feelings, assumptions, past experiences, and prejudices.

3 Barriers between Listener and Speaker

I concentrate on listening actively in every discussion.
Alan Lakien,
"How to Get Control of Your
Time and Your Life"

When one of my grandchildren was five years old, she said to me, "Everybody's got problems, don't they?"

"Yes, I think most people do," I replied.

(Sigh)

"Do you have a problem?" I asked gently.

"Yes."

"What's your problem, Dana?"

"Well . . . my problem is, I don't listen."

"How do you know you don't listen?"

"The teacher was reading a story the other day, and when she stopped she asked each kid if we could tell her what she said. When it came to my turn, I couldn't tell her."

"Hmmm. Well . . . what were you doing when the teacher was reading the story?"

Short pause . . . "I was thinking about something else."

Listening to five-year-olds can be an education! Not many adults realize they have listening problems. When they do stop to think about what they do when they don't listen, adults manage to identify quite a few habits—mostly variations on "thinking of something else"—that interfere with their listening. Here are some that have been mentioned:

"I have a tendency to be too concerned with how people see me."

"I don't listen things out, I just jump in before the other person is through."

"My mind wanders to things I think are most relevant."

"When I'm bored as I listen, I fantasize, do my own thing, or am critical of what's going on."

"Sometimes I stop listening when I become more interested in the speaker's physical features than in what the person is saying."

"Where the subject is of personal interest, I anticipate and wait for the other to stop so I can argue my idea. If I become impatient, I interrupt."

"I'm thinking ahead to what I will say next."

"I'm trying so hard to look interested in what the other person is saying that I don't even hear the words."

"I turn off if the voice is too loud or unpleasant, if one person in the group monopolizes the conversation, or if I'm not interested in the subject of the person talking."

"I judge the speaker, and my listening depends on my judgment."

Which of these habits do you identify with? Most people identify with at least three or four.

Being aware of habits can help people to stop them.

EXERCISE 3.1

To increase your awareness of the ways in which you listen, answer the following questions:

1. When you are bored with what is going on in a discussion or meeting, how do you usually listen?

2. When you are annoyed with another person with whom you want to build a better working relationship, how do you usually listen?

3. Your boss asks you to do something you are uncertain about being able to do well. You also want to hide the fact that you feel inadequate. How effectively do you think you would listen in this situation?

Taking time to reflect on listening behavior by exploring the questions and the listening habits of others is a way to overcome the barriers you may have. Awareness is a vital first step; it is difficult to change something we are not aware of.

The following exercise will help you become aware of listening barriers. The statements reflect many of the processes during communication that influence listening effectiveness.

**LISTENING
ASSESSMENT
EXERCISE**

DIRECTIONS: Mark each statement true or false.

_____　1. People tend to pay attention to what interests them.

_____　2. People tend to expect or anticipate what they are familiar with.

_____　3. Sometimes people distort things so they hear what they want to hear.

_____ 4. Listening is a natural process.

_____ 5. A person's training, experience, and knowledge affect what that person perceives.

_____ 6. Hearing and listening are the same.

_____ 7. Listening is a skill.

_____ 8. Most people have a short attention span and have difficulty concentrating on the same thing for too long.

_____ 9. Listening requires little energy; it is "easy."

_____ 10. The speaker is totally responsible for the success of communication.

_____ 11. An effective listener keeps an open, curious mind.

_____ 12. Speaking is a more important part of the communication process than listening.

_____ 13. When a listener's emotional level is high, he or she will be an effective listener.

_____ 14. When a person is involved with internal distractions, he or she will not be able to listen to what the speaker says.

_____ 15. Being critical and judging a speaker is not an effective listening skill.

Compare your answers with those that follow.

15. T	12. F	9. F	6. F	3. T
14. T	11. T	8. T	5. T	2. T
13. F	10. F	7. T	4. F	1. T

How did you do? I would imagine that most of your answers were correct. By reading two chapters about listening and from your own experience, you have already raised your awareness about factors interfering with effective listening. The statements in the quiz are dealt with more fully throughout the remainder of this chapter.

THE MYTH THAT ONLY SPEAKING PRESENTS POWER

One major barrier to effective listening is that, in this society, we have equated speaking with mastery and power. Talking is used to gain power (political speech, selling a client a product, selling an idea, or persuading someone to agree with you), to punish (arguments, verbal attacks), to relax (dinner talk, social, humorous comments), and to conceal or reveal (employees concealing ideas or holding back what they feel). Not talking to someone is punishment, and so is not listening.

Resistance to listening tends to be our cultural norm. We are often taught that speaking represents action and power, whereas listening connotes weakness and apathy. Personal, competitive needs interfere with taking the time to listen. This kind of thinking results in a negative attitude toward listening, which is often identified as a passive and compliant act.

Listening may be thought of as a passive and compliant act by people, but how many times have you been affected by how a person listened to you? How do you feel when listeners are not paying attention to you by looking at their watches, doing some activity, or not acknowledging what you've said? My guess is you feel like you are talking to a wall. This kind of listening has negative power.

Then there are other times when a person pays attention to you by having good eye contact, is attentive to what you are saying, or acknowledges you. This kind of listening has positive power.

PERCEPTION-RECEPTION-ATTENTION

Listening is a highly selective, subjective experience. Information that conflicts with the listener's present ideas and beliefs may simply be tuned out. When we expect to hear certain things, we don't listen to what is really said. Present in each situation is perception, reception, and attention. Depending on the situation and the listener's motives, different mental interactions between these three and the listener may be activated.

It is important to realize that both the talker and the listener have power. When we ignore the importance of listening, we do a disservice to the value of listening. For example, our perception about a person, a situation, or a subject can influence our reception and how much we will pay attention. We sometimes only pay attention to what interests us or what we like about the talker. On the other hand, the more we are receptive to people or to their point of view because of our positive per-

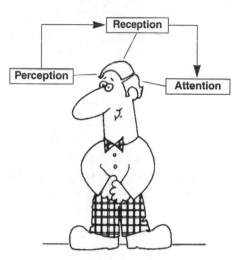

ceptions, the more we will pay attention to what they say. In other words, if our perceptions are positive and nonjudgmental, we will be more receptive to what is going on or being said, which in turn increases our interest.

When I am with a group of people in a training seminar who are interested in the subject I'm presenting because of positive perceptions, they are open to more of the concepts and ideas. They will more than likely act on these ideas for their own personal improvement. The more important the subject is to them, the more listening involvement they get into. In other words, the more relevant my material is to their personal or professional goals—what they want to get out of life or what they want to prove to themselves—the more they listen to what I have to say and the less they tune me out. As mentioned in Chapter 2, one of the filters to listening is values. What a person values will, in turn, influence how attentive and receptive he or she will be. For instance, if I am discussing ways to improve one's ability to communicate more effectively through increased listening skills and a person doesn't see the value in doing this or doesn't care, very little of what I say will be listened to.

It also follows that when groups aren't particularly interested in the subject or disagree with what I say, they tend to gradually pay less attention to what is said. We tend to disregard people who are speaking from a conflicting viewpoint. We often ignore those we don't like or don't respect, even though what they have to say may be important and necessary to get our jobs done.

These factors—perception, reception, attention—happen unconsciously. Often, people aren't aware of the internal process that distracts them from listening at level 1. Once we pay attention to what the speaker is saying, because of a positive perception, our feelings about it and the way it sounds to us will influence our reception of and attention to what is being said. When you feel good about what is said, and it makes sense to you or sounds right, you are receiving the information through your five senses. Using your five senses allows you to get fully involved with the information and be open to listening at level 1. Even smell and taste affect how and what we listen to. For example, have you ever tried to listen to someone with bad breath, body odor, or while eating something you find really delicious or distasteful?

Factors such as the information not sounding good, not making sense or not ringing true act as filters because they are the result of values and past experiences. These filters result in a closed mind. Have you ever talked to someone with a closed mind? Worse than talking to a wall, isn't it? Listeners with closed minds focus on disagreeing, on what is not right, or on what is wrong. This negative process can be a discouraging experience for the talker.

A closed mind often results in the "Yes, but . . ." interaction that might sound something like this conversation between two co-workers:

Jim: I just don't know what I'm going to do about my boss. He's always picking on me for little things I do that he says are wrong.

Dave: You should talk to him about why you're upset.

Jim: Yeah, but I couldn't do that. He'd make life miserable for me.

Dave: Well, you ought to ignore him and not let him bother you.

Jim: Yeah, but then I'd be letting him get away with his lousy behavior and he'd never change.

Dave: Well . . . you should quit and get another job.

Jim: Yeah, but I need the money, and the way the job market is these days I probably wouldn't be able to find another job for months!

Dave: (By this time completely exasperated) Why don't you take out a gun and shoot him!

Notice that each time Dave came up with a solution, Jim spent his listening time thinking of rebuttals to what Dave was suggesting—zeroing in on what wouldn't work. Instead of being open to what Dave suggested and how he might use his suggestions, Jim used his listening time to think of reasons why he couldn't use them. This listening pattern is often perceived as two people going around in circles, and it certainly feels that way to the listener. The problem doesn't get resolved, and the person providing the solutions feels discouraged.

In Chapter 2, I suggested that advice giving often leads to the rescuer behavior mode. Giving solutions or advice is a double-edged problem. As the preceding example illustrated, giving solutions can lead to the "yes . . . but" interchange, and the rescuer mode can lead to the victim mode.

Being a resource person and effective listener instead of an advice giver usually works best with those who ask for help and then discount suggestions. You might change to the summarizing technique, as illustrated in the following example:

Jim: I just don't know what I'm going to do about my boss. He's always picking on me for little things I do that he says are wrong.

Dave: Sounds like you don't know how to handle your boss when he points out things you do that he doesn't like.

Jim: Yeah, he does it a lot. I don't want to tell him about it because it might make him mad; then he'd probably make life miserable for me.

Dave: Hmmm! Seems like you are caught in a double bind. On the one hand, you want to tell your boss what you don't like, and on the other hand, you don't want to tell him because he might get upset with you.

Jim: Yeah! That's exactly what I feel.

Dave: It's a tough spot to be in. What kind of options do you have?

Notice that a summary of what Jim said led to agreement on what was happening, in contrast to the preceding example where Jim and Dave disagreed. Also, the summarizing of Jim's feelings and position helped him see more clearly what was going on between him and his boss.

By being an effective listener, Dave stayed out of the "yes . . . but" interchange, and by not giving advice, he didn't become a rescuer. Dave and Jim have not solved Jim's problem, but at least they have made progress toward a solution. When Dave provided support and assisted Jim in talking through the problem, he laid the groundwork for possible future solutions that might have been impossible because of a closed mind on Jim's part.

HEARING WHAT YOU WANT TO HEAR

As you discovered in the preceding quiz, a listening barrier exists when someone hears what he wants to hear, not what is really communicated. Barriers to listening happen because of one or several filters. For example, past experience filters can make a listener become anxious to hear something that fulfills his or her wishes or desires.

This often happens in business settings, where one person is selling merchandise to another and the salesperson wants the sale to be as large as possible. Jeanne related this story:

> I was working on the order desk for a company that supplied materials for large conferences. One week before, my supervisor had checked with a client about how many packets they needed for their program. She was told that they had only eight registrants. However, they expected more, and she was asked to check back with them.
>
> My supervisor was called out of town, and I was asked to follow up on this client. Well . . . I checked with them for the number of registrants they had now. The client told me eighteen. In my desire to sell the most materials possible, I heard eighty.
>
> Three of us spent three hours getting the materials ready. When the delivery man brought the materials to the client, he was told they only needed eighteen packets, not the eighty we had prepared. I could have fallen through the floor when he told me. I was so embarrassed!

Jeanne expected to hear a larger number because of her anticipation and desire to fill a large order. This caused her to hear incorrectly. As a result, the company lost three hours of work by three people. Jeanne could have avoided a loss of three hours of work, and a great deal of embarrassment, had she used the clarifying technique. When the client said how many packets they wanted she could have said, "Let me make sure how many packets you want delivered, was the number eighty?"

The client would have corrected her right then and there, and the problem would never had occurred.

BIASED LISTENING

Another block to listening occurs when we form an opinion about the level and value of what will be said. We label the information ahead of time as unimportant, too boring, too complex, or nothing new, and we are anxious for the speaker to get to the point.

Our listening can be biased because of a negative experience we had with a person we are communicating with. We can often let our negative past experiences filter through into a present situation. These negative past experiences are held subconsciously in our heads. This results in biased listening because we aren't totally in the here and now with that person. Steven related this example:

> I have a technician from another department who takes what seems forever to return my calls. These calls have to do with information I need to complete my part of the projects we are both working on. Instead of bringing up my frustration to him directly, I let my feelings burn inside of me, mainly my stomach. Whenever we were in a project meeting I wouldn't listen to him. As a result I missed hearing important details; then I'd have to call him to get those missed details. Talk about putting myself in a no win situation. I guess it's time for me to bring up the issue and work it through.

As you can see from the examples above, a biased listener tends to distort the message positively or negatively, often getting so emotionally involved that listening efficiency suffers. Certain emotionally laden words, sometimes referred to as "red flag" or "buzz" words, can evoke strong feelings and thus create barriers to effective listening. We sometimes respond to a word or phrase in a way that has been conditioned by our past experiences. In other words, we have attached meanings to the same word from prior, emotion-laden situations. Sometimes words can affect listeners to such an extent that their reactions will result in level 3 listening, as their emotions are causing internal distractions to occur, thus interfering with level 1 listening. Unconsciously, we tune out what we negatively label.

EXERCISE 3.2

Following are some words that may be emotionally charged. Take a moment to check the ones that are red flag words for you, and add any others you have found that have an emotional impact on people.

_____ You should, have to, have got to, are supposed to, must

_____ You're a failure,

_____ Slowpoke

_____ Stupid, dumb

_____ I demand

_____ Everytime you

_____ You do this all the time.

_____ Rude

_____ Irresponsible

_____ You lack

_____ Your weaknesses are

_____ You never, always

_____ You fail to understand.

_____ You claim

_____ You are confused.

_____ Sissy

_____ Thoughtless

Now that you have checked your red flag words, think for a moment about what happens when one of these words is said to you. What internal process do you go through? In other words, what are the ramifications of these words on your behavior?

Do your reactions match any of the following examples? If so, check the ones that do and then develop an affirmative plan to deal with the behavior pattern as you did in Chapter 1, page 19.

_____ I say to myself, "He's right, I'm stupid, I guess I'll never be able to get things done right."

_____ "Who is she to talk to me that way? I'll show her."

_____ I stop thinking and my emotions take over, which interferes with my listening to much of what the other person is saying.

_____ I become defensive and start thinking of ways to justify my behavior.

_____ I identify with my negative behavior or mistake and feel that I'm bad and really "not OK."

_____ I'm puzzled by what he is saying. I think of the most appropriate response to make in order to stay in charge of my feelings and the interactions.

People resent being judged and labeled negatively, and being given no choice in deciding their own actions. Often, these words and phrases result in lack of cooperation and motivation.

Anna had a supervisor who told her what she "should" and "had to" do, without allowing Anna to offer alternative courses of action. One time, Anna suggested another way to do a job she had learned in another company that would save time. Her supervisor, without discussing it further, ignored her suggestion and said, "This is the way we do it around here, and if you want to make it in this company, you'll do as you're told!" Anna's response was, "I really had to fight so that my emotions wouldn't influence the way I did my job. I felt that I was treated like a child and wasn't given an opportunity to think things out for myself or solve my own problems."

Every day words provoke different feelings or ideas in different people. These emotion-laden words often have a strong impact on people that interferes with listening. Tones of voice have the same kind of impact.

EXERCISE 3.3

Become aware of yourself the next time you begin to feel angry or tense in response to one of your red flag words or tones of voice. Get in touch with your emotional state and how it influences your behavior and ability to listen. Be aware that you probably won't listen to the message accurately.

1. Recall the word, tone of voice, who said it, and in what kind of situation.

2. Bring back into your consciousness, as vividly as possible, the emotion you felt when you heard that word or tone of voice. What emotion did you feel?

3. Now analyze the connection between the word or tone of voice and your feelings about it. What connection did you discover?

EXERCISE 3.3
(continued)

4. After you established this connection, think of two different contexts in which the words or tone of voice could be used that would change the meaning. You will find when you do this that the effect on you will be different.

Understanding how words, because of your previous experience, affect your biases can help you be more in charge of yourself the next time they are spoken.

GREEN FLAG WORDS

A variation of this phenomenon is the manner in which positive words can also effect an emotional response in us that can interfere with our listening. For example, imagine yourself listening to someone who has just said that you have done something successfully, that your approach was right on target, and then . . . goes on to give you some additional information about how you are to implement the procedure. You could be so busy responding positively to the statements made about you that you wouldn't listen to what the person is saying about implementing the procedure.

It appears that positive words as well as negative ones have an impact on our listening behavior. Whenever a word, phrase, or topic elicits an emotional response from us, there is a chance that what follows will not be listened to at level 1. As demonstrated by Jeff's experience:

I'm a salesman for a large software company. We sell complex customized software systems to large corporations. When I had only been on the job six months I got the go-ahead to have installed a very expensive complex system for a Fortune 1,000 company. Needless to say, I was very excited about getting the sale. When the company employee stated two specifications to the program they wanted done, I didn't listen effectively. I proceeded to write up the contract without these two specifications. Thank goodness, I have a savvy and knowledgeable manager. She remembered from one of our meetings with the client that they had asked about a specification. So she questioned me about it. To make a long story short, I went back to the client to find out about any specifications they wanted and listened very carefully to what was said.

Jeff learned a very valuable lesson—listen at level 1 in all situations. It is easy to think because a situation is positive it is not necessary to listen at level 1.

THE EFFECTS OF EMOTIONS ON LISTENING

Along with words that affect our biases that lead to emotions, there are some areas we do not want to talk about, topics that we have an emotional reason for not wanting to discuss. These areas are also "hot buttons" for us. When another person pushes our hot button with a word, phrase, or topic, our mind goes through certain filters: past experiences, beliefs, or biases connected to what the other is saying. As a defensive measure, we often tune out the talker, plan rebuttals, or formulate questions to confuse the talker.

If something is said that might cause us to change our perception, we feel threatened. Potential change in our perceptions can involve strong feelings. Often, the first feelings are frustration and confusion. To reduce these feelings, we flee mentally from what is being said by turning out what the talker is saying or by distorting it so we won't have to alter our perception, belief, or opinion.

Experiencing high emotions, either positive or negative, usually interferes with listening ability. Strong feelings are one barrier that influences effective listening, and they sometimes cause confusion and the taking in of information in a disorganized manner, as illustrated by June's experience:

I'm a caseworker, which means I deal with people who come into our agency for help finding a job. I was so sympathetic to what they were saying, I became overly emotional and found it difficult to think objectively. When I did this, I couldn't think effectively and didn't obtain all the information I needed to match the client to the proper job.

"I heard every word you said."

June had developed a habit of listening almost entirely with her feelings. As a result, she was not taking in the kinds of information she needed to get her job done properly. She often became overanxious, which accelerated her tension level.

STYLES OF LISTENING

The Faker

Some people fake attention. They pretend to listen when their minds are actually off on a flashing tangent. They may fake attention because they think they are pleasing the talker. Often, people who wish to be attentive have their eyes riveted on the talker. Their ears appear to be wide open. They so exhaust themselves in playing the attentive role that they end up no longer listening at all. Have you ever watched a person fake listening by smiling and head-nodding, when neither the smile nor the head-nodding matched what the talker was saying?

Others try hard to fake being good listeners by trying to memorize every fact given; thus, the intent of the message becomes lost. However, they give the impression of listening with interest and curiosity. This need to hear and digest everything being said can easily lead to an overloading and jamming of the communication network.

The Dependent Listener

Some listeners are highly dependent and live vicariously through the opinions, wishes, and feelings of others. Often, their feelings are evoked in interpersonal communication situations, making it difficult for them to deal with abstract matters. So much concern is given to how they are listening and reacting to the talker that they miss out on what is actually being said. In their urgency to elicit a favorable impression from the talker, they focus on how they appear to others, rather than on the clarity and content of what they are saying.

> Norman's father dominated his relationships when he was young. He often told Norman, "Children should be seen and not heard." When Norman expressed an opinion on a subject, his father told him he was stupid and not old enough to know the right way to do things. In their interactions, Norman's father would often say, "You'd better listen to every word I'm saying, young man!"
> As a result of this communication, Norman became a dependent listener. He put his effort into appearing to listen in order to please others. He often felt confused and frustrated. He also felt like a doormat because he went along with other people's wishes at the expense of his own. He discovered he didn't have many opinions of his own because he let others do his talking for him. In his relationships with his co-workers, he was afraid to say no. This behavior pattern resulted in his feeling tense, unhappy, and victimized.

The Interrupter   Sam had a habit of interrupting when others were talking. He thought he'd forget what he wanted to say if he didn't interrupt. He often felt anxious if he wasn't able to say what was on his mind. Many times, the people he worked with became frustrated and annoyed by his behavior.

While completing a self-awareness exercise, he discovered he was so busy focusing on what he wanted to say that he listened at level 2 or 3. In the process, he wasn't considering the talker's needs. During a practice session, in which he had to paraphrase what the other said, he became conscious of his internal process. He started to think of what he wanted to say after the talker had spoken only a few words. After he became aware of this internal process, he could stop and direct his attention to what the talker was saying. He found he could remember what he wanted to say by associating what the talker had said with the information he wanted to discuss.

Bringing up something that doesn't relate to what the talker is saying is another form of interruption. Often, this is done when the talker is discussing something the listener is uncomfortable with and feels threatened by. The listener takes the conversation off on unrelated tangents as a means to sidestep the issue being discussed. The talker gets so involved in the side issue that the real issue is never dealt with.

Paul had an employee, Fred, who came late to work three to four times a week. Paul had approached Fred about his lateness on several occasions. He became discouraged because the conversations ended up going around in a circle.

Paul: You came in fifteen minutes late again this morning. You should be on time.

Fred: I'm a good worker, and I've been with the company ten years.

Paul: I think you're a good worker, too, but you have to be at work on time. That's the rule!

Fred: I can't do everything right. I keep trying to get to work on time, but I just can't seem to do it. Anyway, I get my work done.

Paul: Why don't you get up earlier in the morning as I told you to!

Fred: I try to, but I can't. Anyway, Janet over there takes longer breaks than I do. I don't know why you only pick on me.

Paul: I don't think Janet takes longer breaks than anyone else in the office. I don't pick only on you. When others infringe on the rules, I talk to them, too. Can you try to get to work on time from now on?

Fred: Yeah, I'll try.

This can be a discouraging and frustrating experience, yet it happens often. Problems don't get resolved when one person is able to sidetrack the real problem. When you find yourself in this situation, a couple of statements can be used.

For example, when Fred said, "I'm a good worker, and I've been with the company ten years," Paul could have said, "I appreciate your good work and time with the company, but that's not the reason for this discussion. The issue is your lateness. I want it to stop, and I want to know how you are going to end this situation."

Or, when Fred said, "Anyway, Janet over there takes longer breaks than I do," Paul might have said, "That's not the issue here," or, "That's not relevant to our discussion; we are talking about your lateness," or, "Right now I'm only concerned about your lateness."

By using such statements, Paul could control the discussion *and* move the interaction to a solution.

The Self-Conscious Listener

Some individuals focus too much attention on themselves by thinking, "Am I doing well or badly?"; "Do I look all right?"; or, "I wonder if the talker thinks I'm intelligent?" These people give attention to themselves as participants when it would be better to involve themselves in the content and meaning of the conversation.

Self-consciousness can also be viewed as a kind of preoccupation with internal matters at the expense of effective listening. When people become too concerned about how well the discussion is going, they often lose their spontaneity and become overly involved with themselves during the conversation. Our society has unspecified standards as to how much people are allowed to be carried away by talk and how thoroughly they are to permit themselves to be caught up in the conversation. People who become too involved give the impression that they don't have self-control over their feelings and actions. This can lead the listener to draw away from involvement with the other person. One person's overeagerness can be another's alienation. In this kind of situation, the talker is forced to adjust to the listener's state of emotion because the listener is incapable of adjusting his or her own.

The Intellectual or Logical Listener

The intellectual listeners listen mostly with their heads, hearing only what they want to hear, blotting out larger areas of reality. Because they are mainly interested in a rational appraisal, perhaps as a result of their educational training, they tend to neglect the emotional and nonverbal aspects of the talker's behavior. Thus, they listen at level 2, only to the words, rather than the whole message. Their evaluation of what is said is most often geared to the interpretation of verbal statements, often causing them to miss the less obvious intent.

They are not aware of how listening behavior affects others or how others affect them. They listen in terms of categories, making certain that what they listen to does not disturb their inner peace or systematic order. It is almost as if they are putting what the talker is saying into a computer's data bank. If a statement doesn't fit into a systematic logical sequence, their minds reject what is said as invalid. I refer to this process as getting into "analysis paralysis."

These types of listeners are so involved in programming what is being said that they miss out on the deeper meaning of what is spoken. These types of listeners cut off experiencing through the sensory system, thus losing the opportunity to actually experience the event. The brain is so busy making calculations that the body isn't given the chance to feel the communication. As a result, nonverbal communication is disregarded. All this is happening because the listeners are blind to their own emotions and the emotions of others.

Frank was a computer programmer whose job demanded that he analyze information, focusing on what might be wrong or how a program could be improved. To succeed at his work, he had to pick information apart, listen to what could go wrong, and compute information in a logical systematic manner.

He was so busy analyzing what was communicated to him, he didn't have time to just be there with the other person. His wife often told him he was a nit-picker. She felt he was overly critical of her and the children because he seldom accepted what she said. He would challenge her thought processes. He spent most of their communication time analyzing what she said as if he had to turn it into a program.

This listening pattern had a serious effect on his marriage and social life. After becoming aware of the pattern, he took steps to change it outside of his job. It took a lot of concentration and effort to change this pattern, but he said it was more than worth it.

PHYSICAL BARRIERS

The last internal barrier we will cover is the physical barrier: what happens physically that influences an individual's listening efficiency. At certain *times of the day,* we have more energy than at others. *Fatigue* is a factor in listening, since listening takes concentration and effort. When we don't feel up to par, we have a more difficult time being attentive.

It is easier to daydream and become preoccupied when our energy level is low. When we have personal problems, our energy is often used to deal with the problems, which lessens the amount of energy we have available to listen at level 1. Personal problems sometimes manage to creep into our minds while someone else is talking.

Another element that can cause fatigue is the "time-lag factor"; the average talker speaks about 200 words per minute, but a listener can process information at around 300 to 500 words per minute. It is easy to spend this time lag daydreaming, going on mental tangents, and thinking of personal problems. It takes energy to use this time difference for more productive use, such as internally summarizing what the person said, visualizing what is being said, or associating what is being said with something already stated. Because level 2 listening takes energy and concentration, it is easy to allow these factors to interfere with it.

The fatigue barrier is often prevalent during meetings, especially those held at the end of the day or in the evening. People attending have already expended considerable energy getting the day's work done. Along with this low-energy factor, listening at meetings can be boring. Most often, the agenda does not have the same interest for all those who are attending.

In this case, it would be important to listen at level 2 to make sure you aren't missing information you will need. If what is being said pertains to you, you could then move to level 1, in which you would process the information. You might even want to jot down some notes to be used later as memory triggers.

SEMANTIC BARRIER: THE MEANINGS ARE IN PEOPLE, NOT WORDS

We each have our own meanings for words because we filter them through our varied beliefs, knowledge, education, upbringing, and experience. As a result, no two people have exactly the same meaning for the same word or expression; meanings are not in words, meanings are in people.

The dictionary contains thousands of words. However, the average adult uses about 500 of these words most often, and each has between 20 and 25 meanings! So, two people can use 500 words with the possibility of 12,500 different meanings!

A word is simply a representation of the thing it names or describes. It is not the thing itself, and may mean something different to the talker than it does to the listener. The practice of summarizing what you believe the talker said, as a check, can ensure understanding.

We make judgments about people based on how we understand what we see and perceive. We evaluate an individual's competence and motivation through our semantic filters.

Have you ever tried to moderate between two people who are arguing, and have had to say, "Wait a minute, he didn't say what you said he said." Usually, people do not purposely change what people say; they simply do not hear the same words in the same way that the words were said. I have a sign that I display in my seminars which reads: "I know you believe you understand what I said, but I'm not sure you realize that what you heard is not what I meant." Everyone receives sensory data in a unique way; it is not "raw" data, but rather, data that is filtered and interrupted by the receiver.

Karen had this example to share in a listening seminar.

Last week, when we talked about and practiced the summarizing technique, I thought to myself, 'I bet that's something I can do in our meeting tomorrow.' I did the summarizing technique four times during the meeting. I was amazed about how much I assume. Each time, if I hadn't summarized, I would have come away from the meeting with faulty information.

What Karen reported is what goes on in every meeting in Corporate America. Imagine the loss in time, misunderstandings, wrong action, and increased stress that poor listening causes!

EXERCISE 3.4

Take a few moments to examine the following pictures. Jot down the words that best describe the meaning you see in the facial expressions, body postures, and gestures of each of the people in these pictures.

Now, ask another person to do the same without letting him or her see your answers. Compare the answers. How similar are they?

How different?

It is important to recognize that the statements we make about others, after we listen to them, are statements about our own experience. Sometimes people have a difficult time separating external reality from their own experience because of filters.

CAN YOU SEPARATE EXTERNAL REALITY FROM EXPERIENCE?

Imagine that the statements that follow have been spoken by another person. Can you distinguish between those portions that actually took place in external reality and those that happened only in this person's internal experience?

EXERCISE 3.5

Mark an X in the parentheses if the statement contains a description of only what happened externally. Underline all parts that are interpreted through the speaker's internal experience.

( ) 1. Carl waited patiently as he stood at the counter reading a magazine.

( ) 2. I saw people being thoughtless and lacking in sensitivity.

( ) 3. The man turned off the car lights and walked into a blue house.

Of the three, only the third statement strictly describes external reality (the behavior of the man). In the first item, "waited patiently" is a judgment of the observer. Also, "reading a magazine" presumes an internal process that cannot be seen. Carl could actually have been holding a magazine while thinking about his financial troubles or his golf game.

In the second item, "thoughtless and lacking in sensitivity" cannot be observed in external reality. This is an opinion of the observer based on other things he saw the people doing, observations that are not described in the statement. Each set of filters influences how each individual makes sense of his reality. Can you imagine the problems this process has for our listening efficiency!

Geri worked for an agency as a counter representative. After she completed an exercise similar to the one you just completed, she shared this story about herself:

> I didn't realize, until now, how often I quickly put faulty interpretations on what people did and said. I discovered how quickly I judge people, based on my own beliefs about what people should or should not do. As our group was discussing the results of this exercise, I realized what I had been doing. The other day, I felt anxious and frustrated when I was dealing with a male client. During our discussion, he kept squinting at me, frowning, and talking loudly to me. I became very nervous working with him, because I believed he shouldn't treat me that way. My nervousness changed to anger the more he frowned at me. About halfway through our transactions, his daughter came in. She had had a difficult time finding a parking place and, as a result, was late getting to our office. She had come with her father to help him with his claim. She told me he had lost his glasses, had difficulty seeing close, and was hard of hearing! What I put myself through by misinterpreting that man's behavior!

EXTERNAL DISTRACTIONS

So far we have been talking about internal distractions—things people do internally to build barriers that prevent them from listening effectively. External factors can also interfere with effective listening. Following are some factors that may be external barriers. Put a check by those that affect you.

____ Talker not speaking loudly enough, or whispering

____ Talker's mannerisms, appearance

___ Loud noises, such as traffic, machinery

___ Room temperature too hot or too cold

___ Faulty acoustics, making it difficult to hear

___ Views of outside activity or scenery

___ Clock-watching

___ Interruptions, phone calls

___ Talker speaking in a monotone or an unfamiliar accent, or talking too rapidly or too slowly

___ Time pressure, deadlines

___ Work pressures, taking on more than one can handle, doing two or three things at one time

"You're not listening!"

The following may also impair the ability to listen. Check those things you recognize as ones that impair yours (add any others not listed).

___ Fidgeting

___ Doodling

___ Stormy weather

___ Chewing gum

___ Color combinations on the wall

___ Being seated among people you don't know

_____ Tapping foot or pencil

_____ Picking up something, a magazine, or a book

_____ Other

THE IMPORTANCE OF LISTENING TO NONVERBALS

Much is communicated that isn't verbalized! Even when an individual is not talking, he is still communicating in some manner. One of the most important skills of effective listening is listening to nonverbals.

Recent studies reveal three major categories that influence those who are involved in the communication process. Circle the percentage number shown in Figure 3.1 that you think represents the correct percentage for each category.

These figures of 7 percent for words, 38 percent for vocal (tone of voice), and 55 percent for facial expressions, posture, eye contact, and gestures were quoted in a widely read article by Albert Mehrabian.[6] Another prominent authority, Randall Harrison, claims that a mere 35 percent of the meaning of a communication comes from words; the remainder comes from body language.[7] You may question the specific percentages reached by these researchers. However, you probably don't dispute the general direction of their findings. Earlier, I mentioned how my frowning expression affected others negatively. The nonverbals are indeed significant in the listening process. Think of the times people have influenced you simply by the way they looked at you.

Close observation will reveal how much people convey through facial expressions. Watch face color and how it changes as people talk about things they have feelings about. Movements of the lips, mouth, cheek

FIGURE 3.1

What is the impact of each aspect of communication?

	Relative Impact (Approximate)			
	A	B	C	D
Words (verbal)	30%	7%	16%	42%
Vocal (tone)	40%	27%	38%	10%
Body Language:				
Facial Expressions, Posture, Gestures, Eye Contact	20%	55%	32%	40%

muscles, and eyebrows can provide illuminating data about what is going on internally with the person you are listening to. Become aware of expressions that convey tension, doubt, trust, inattention, and so forth.

Listening to the emotional tone of a talker is another skill that can assist you in being aware of feelings not expressed verbally. The tone of voice can convey attitudes that can be a clue about how to deal with a person in a difficult situation. The nonverbal aspect of the communication process is largely unconscious and less likely to be manipulated or disguised by the individual.

The skilled listener hears more than the speaker's words. He listens to the pitch, rate, timbre, and subtle variations that the tone of voice is communicating. A manager told me that when an employee enters his office, he often asks himself, "What does the voice say when I stop listening to the words and listen only to the voice tone and inflection?"

A supervisor, George, was complaining to a seminar group that the employees he supervised weren't motivated. They wouldn't do more than they had to. I had a pretty good idea why, along with the rest of the group. He had a rasping voice that had a jangling effect on me. (As it turned out, others felt the same way.) His eye contact was piercing and penetrating, and his overall manner was pushy and demanding. I asked him if he gave positive feedback to the people he supervised or expressed his appreciation of a job well done. He said, "Certainly," and proceeded to demonstrate how he did this by role playing with another participant, Steve.

When George walked abruptly toward Steve and delivered his comment in his rasping voice, Steve reacted by leaning back, folding his arms, and looking at George grimly.

I asked Steve how George's delivery affected him. When he described to George how his delivery came across to him, George listened in disbelief. He looked around the room at the other participants, expecting them to disagree with Steve. When everyone in the room stated that they were affected in about the same way as Steve, George sat down heavily. I could see the struggle going on within him. He squirmed in his chair and a look of confusion was on his face.

After he had had time to reflect on his experience, he was most appreciative of the group's honest feedback. He was thankful for the opportunity to discover this side of his nonverbal behavior that was influencing others and how they responded to him.

Although most communications will not be as strained as they were for George, all of us tend to forget about the importance of our nonverbal behavior. Like George, we may be blind to it and how it can affect others. George demonstrated a critical factor in terms of awareness and personal growth. Since he was open to listening to our feedback about his nonverbal behavior, he could make a decision to modify it. This was certainly a courageous act, as many people would have difficulty seeing themselves as imperfect and even greater difficulty doing something about it. In the dynamics of the communication process, we affect others without saying a word. We can set a positive or negative tone by how we project nonverbally. Have you ever started to walk up to someone only to stop in your tracks when he or she looked up at you with a certain angry look? Don't forget that you must communicate!

EXERCISE 3.6

Take a moment to reflect on the following questions and write your responses.

What do people do nonverbally to let you know they aren't listening?

To let you know they have a problem?

To let you know nonverbally that they want to terminate the conversation?

To let you know they aren't interested in what is being said?

To let you know they have responded to red flag words?

To let you know they are daydreaming?

Now examine your answers. Do any of them describe your behavior? If there is any behavior you want to change, take a few minutes and write a quick plan of action for how you could begin to modify or change your behavior. Or, if you found some things about yourself that you like, take credit for it and pat yourself on the back.

Plan of Action:

Things I Found Out That I Like About Myself:

What I Want to Modify and/or Improve:

DISCREPANCIES

I once witnessed a conversation in which an employee said to her manager, "You seem irritated with me." The manager's face was flushed red, he clenched his fist, and said harshly, "I'm not angry!" The employee found the manager's body language and his tone of voice more convincing than his words.

The nonverbals make it more difficult to hide what we feel. People may successfully choose words to create a facade, but they are usually fooling only themselves. They may think they have covered their emotions, when unconsciously the emotion is being expressed tonally or through gestures. People can try to camouflage anger with smiles, but tone and body posture will probably give them away.

As you become more skilled at reading and listening to the nonverbals, you will notice that shrugged shoulders are used to convey indifference when, in fact, the issue being discussed is important; a poker face is covering up emotion that is being expressed by tense facial muscles; a quivering lip may indicate an effort to prevent crying; avoiding eye contact may indicate disinterest, dislike, or embarrassment; and eye contact may mean a pretense of interest.

These nonverbals are cues to help you figure out what is going on between you and the other person. It is important to keep in mind that we tend to interpret what we hear and see through our own internal filtering of experience.

For instance, I would caution you against the "mind-reading phenomenon" that often occurs when people imagine what the other person is feeling, based on past experience or faulty misinterpretations. They think their interpretation is truly what the person is feeling when, in fact, it isn't. This happens especially in relationships where people have worked together for a long time.

Sometimes a past experience that was painful and emotionally charged is generalized to other, similar situations. The present experience triggers the memory of the previous situation, which in turn influences the person to interpret the other's behavior through a highly charged, experiential filter, thus reacting to the situation automatically. When one person misreads the intent of the other person's present behavior, communication breaks down.

During the first few months on the job, Kim had made a serious error when doing the books for a small company she worked for. The owner had gotten very angry. His nonverbal behavior included a loud voice, an angry facial expression with his eyebrows pulled together, his arms folded tightly across his chest, and his right foot tapping quickly. Thereafter, whenever the owner portrayed this type of behavior, Kim immediately thought she had done something wrong, felt anxious, and worried that she might lose her job. When it was pointed out to her that she could be interpreting the owner's internal state incorrectly, she decided to talk to him to find out for certain what was going on.

Dennis had a similar experience with a co-worker named Joe. Dennis decided to check with Joe to find out what was going on when he looked at him crossly and seemed angry. Joe was surprised. He didn't realize he had an angry look on his face. He told Dennis that he wasn't even looking at Dennis, but through him. It seems that when Joe is in deep concentration or when something is bothering him about the job, he gets a cross, angry look on his face.

When a person's behavior puzzles you, check with him or her to prevent misunderstanding. You may discover just how often people are blind to their own nonverbal behavior.

BETTER-QUALITY INFORMATION

Level 1 listening can promote better-quality information. When you are listening effectively, you have a better chance of being in charge of a situation and influencing the outcome. By doing this, you know what is being misunderstood and when it is necessary to stop for clarification. Initiating verbal feedback guarantees that you and the talker are using words that mean the same thing. Often we talk in abstract terms. We know what we are saying, but we are describing it to the other person abstractly.

The cartoon in Figure 3.2 shows how communication improves when clarifying questions are used to verify what is being said.

The real tragedy in communication is not the large blunders we make, but the small, unknowing ways in which we cut ourselves off from understanding what happened in the first place. An assumption that has a dangerous effect on communication is that words contain the same meaning and visual images for the talker as they do for the listener. These assumptions—that words contain meaning like a cup holds coffee, and that the speaker uses words that way—probably are two main detriments to effective communication. We are prone to hear what we want to hear.

Using verbal feedback by asking what, when, where, how, who, and why, can reduce misunderstanding and faulty communication or "befuddling."

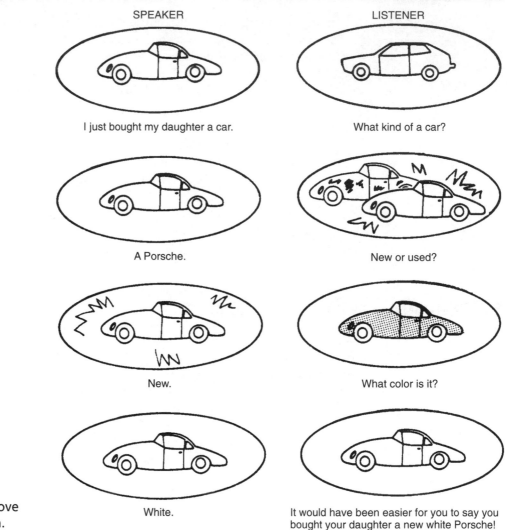

SPEAKER   LISTENER

I just bought my daughter a car.   What kind of a car?

A Porsche.   New or used?

New.   What color is it?

White.   It would have been easier for you to say you bought your daughter a new white Porsche!

FIGURE 3.2
How clarifying questions improve communication.

"Befuddling" is the degree to which verbal communication is misinterpreted, distorted, and filtered out as it passes up, down, and through an organization.

These filters have a tremendous impact on effective listening because each person befuddles to some extent. If befuddling goes on only 34 percent of the time, think of how it impairs the quality of information communicated from one person to another. The befuddling process might look something like the diagram in Figure 3.3.

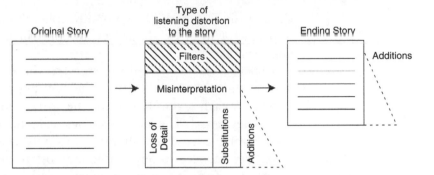

FIGURE 3.3
The "befuddling" process.

To demonstrate this befuddling process, try an exercise called the "rumor chain." You probably remember playing a similar game when you attended elementary school. Divide people into two groups. Each group decides to whom they will listen and tell a story. A person from

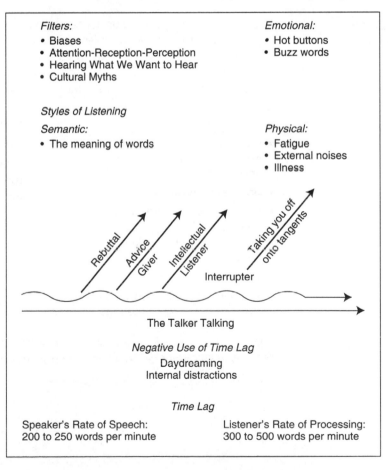

FIGURE 3.4
Barriers to listening.

each group is chosen. These two people are taken away from the group and read a story of about two minutes in length, consisting of about eight sentences.

These two people tell the story to the next person in their group, who in turn relates the story to the next person, and so on, until the last person in each group has heard the story. Then these two people write what they heard. The story becomes distorted to such an extent that the main thought has been almost completely changed; the eight sentences have been reduced to one or two, and often these sentences are additions to the real story. It seems that when people can't make sense out of what is said to them, they make up something that seems logical. Figure 3.4 sums up the barriers that can interfere with effective listening.

PRACTICE SESSION

To practice listening with your new awareness and understanding, do the following exercise with a co-worker, friend, or family member.

With another person, take turns discussing your thoughts, feelings, and ideas on each topic on the numbered list that follows; first one, then the other. While the speaker is talking, the listener is to follow these guidelines:

Do	Do Not
• Listen with understanding, nonjudgmentally, and noncritically	• Interrupt
• Have eye contact	• Fidget
• Face the person with an open, relaxed posture	• Tune out what the other person is saying
• Acknowledge the talker by	
• nodding head	
• leaning forward	
• making facial expressions that match the talker's feelings	

When the instructions tell you to do a listening check, summarize what the talker said by paraphrasing, in your own words, what your partner said.

1. When I meet a person for the first time I . . .

2. I am motivated when . . .

3. My most frequent daydreams are . . .
   Listening Check: What I hear you saying is
   (Summarize what the speaker said about the last topic pertaining to day-dreams.)

4. The way I prefer to get recognition and attention is . . .

5. When I think about the future, I . . .

6. To me, a trusting environment includes . . .
   Listening Check: As I understand it, you . . .
   (Paraphrase in your own words what the speaker said about a trusting environment.)

7. What I like least about my job is . . .

8. What I like best about my job is . . .

9. I am happiest when . . .
   Listening Check: You feel . . .
   (Summarize in your own words what the speaker said; reflect any feelings heard about the last topic.)

10. The thing that bugs me the most is . . .

11. My strongest points are . . .

12. When I am criticized, I usually . . .
    Listening Check: It sounds like . . .
    (Summarize what the speaker said about being criticized.)

13. The emotion I find most difficult to handle is . . .

14. The best way I have found to evaluate my listening habits is . . .

15. The thing I like best about you is . . .

16. I feel . . .
    Listening Check: It seems you . . .
    (Summarize what you thought most important of the last four topics.)

SUMMARY

In this chapter the focus has been on what we do as listeners to cause barriers between ourselves and the people talking to us. You completed a listening quiz that helped you become aware of the kinds of things that affect good listening and what factors show the difference between listening and hearing. The various barriers to effective listening were defined and explained through relevant on-the-job examples and exercises. I identified a variety of barriers that lead to befuddling, such as semantic, physical, filters, emotional, misinterpretation, loss of details, and distortions. You learned how important the nonverbal component of listening is and the importance of listening to the whole message.

SELF-TEST   To test your understanding of the concepts covered in this chapter, take a few minutes to answer the following questions.

1. What are three factors that influence what people listen to?

2. Define *red flag words.*

3. List three of the five styles of listening that interfere with effective listening.

4. What is meant by a semantic barrier?

5. List three of the eight barriers to listening that were described in this chapter.

6. Why is attending to nonverbal behavior important for effective listening?

ANSWERS

1. Perception, reception, attention.

2. Red flag words are emotion-laden words that evoke strong feelings and that can create barriers to listening.

3. The faker, the dependent listener, the interrupter, the self-conscious listener, and the logical listener.

4. The understanding that some people have of one word can differ to other people because of the numerous definitions of that same word.

5. Time lag
    internal distractions—daydreaming, mental tangents, rebuttals
    emotions—red flag and green flag words
    biases
    styles of listening
    semantic
    external
    physical

6. Attending to nonverbal behavior is important because people express much of what they are feeling in this manner. By attending to a person's facial expression and emotional tone, a listener can be more aware of what the talker might be feeling. This is also a way to pick up on discrepancies—when the words are saying one thing while the nonverbal behavior is expressing an emotion that contradicts what is being said.

4 Listening to Yourself

To understand is interesting: winners use their understand-ing to take action.

Howard Newburger and Marjorie Lee,
Winners and Losers

Self-awareness and increased productivity can be achieved through lis-tening to yourself. Often, when people become conscious of how they talk to themselves, they are shocked—shocked at the negative tone of their internal dialogue. This negative dialogue has become a habit. Such automatic responses cause the continuation of nonproductive behaviors that can result in defensiveness, going around in circles, stress, and nonassertiveness. These are the ways in which we lose our power.

It is difficult to understand others until we learn to listen effectively to ourselves. By developing this ability, we can then find ways to develop insight into our on-the-job experiences. Developing the capacity to examine ourselves critically helps us to be aware of our beliefs, values, and attitudes in order to understand and reshape them. By reaching a level of self-acceptance, we then can remain open to our self-defeating behaviors. It is important to listen to ourselves from our heart, nonjudg-mentally—in other words, being our own best friend instead of our own worst enemy. When we assume responsibility for ourselves, following the road to self-development, personal effectiveness, and power can be a privilege rather than a chore.

INTERNAL THOUGHT PROCESS

One way to start listening to yourself is to become aware of your internal thought processes. Developing the habit of listening to what you are thinking is the first step in being more aware of why you feel and behave as you do. This awareness can lead to an understanding of the beliefs by which you live your life. These beliefs may result in the feeling that external forces control your life and that you do not control what you do and feel.

Consider the case of Margie:

Margie is an excellent secretary who works for three engineers. She takes the initiative, thinks problems through to a logical conclusion, works hard, and does everything asked of her. She is experiencing a lot of stress, which manifests itself in stomach problems and insomnia.

When she started to listen to her internal thought process around the issue of stress, she discovered that she was thinking, "As a secretary, my job is to do everything for everybody. I have to keep everyone happy." As a result of this thought process, she said yes to every request. She often overcommitted herself, said yes to tasks that weren't really her responsibility, and often worked overtime and on weekends, causing family problems, feelings of resentment, and missed deadlines.

Instead of being pleased with her industriousness, the three engineers started to complain about the missed deadlines. Margie felt unappreciated and used. Her motivation decreased. She became irritable and took time off from work to "teach them a lesson!" Thus, she got farther behind in her work, felt more pressured, and received more criticism from the engineers: a never-ending cycle!

GOING NOWHERE CYCLE

Because Margie wasn't listening to her internal thought process in relation to her stressful situation, she was stuck in a "Going Nowhere

Situation →	Thought Process →	Behavior →	Feelings
An engineer asks her to do a task she can't complete on time if she is to finish what she is presently working on.	"I have to do everything for everybody—I have to keep everybody happy."	• Being passive, saying yes when she would like to say no • Overcommitting herself • Tension, irritability.	• Resentment • Irritation • Frustration • Pressure

FIGURE 4.1

Margie's Going Nowhere Cycle.

Cycle." She didn't examine the thoughts that caused here to behave this way. Since Margie was unaware of this process, she continued the self-defeating behavior that resulted in feelings of resentment, irritation and frustration. Margie's Going Nowhere Cycle is shown in Figure 4.1.

When Margie learned to listen to her internal thought process, she saw and understood how her Going Nowhere Cycle kept her stuck in stressful behavior. Because she learned to listen to what she said internally to cause her own stress and negative feelings, she was able to do something about it. She was surprised that she could actually hear a voice inside her head saying, "I have to do everything for everybody—I have to keep everybody happy." This awareness led her to choose to modify her internal thought process, a modification that moved her from a negative to a positive internal dialogue.

She found out this internal Going Nowhere Cycle influenced her to experience the victim mode in the drama triangle. By behaving from the belief that "she had to do everything for everybody," Margie often felt others were persecuting her by making their demands. Until she took the time to listen to her Going Nowhere internal dialogue, she did not realize that she was the person responsible for putting unrealistic demands on herself that led to her experiencing the feeling of being a victim.

GOING SOMEWHERE CYCLE

Margie's modified cycle helped her deal with others more assertively. The new thought process had a positive effect on her performance that resulted in her getting her work done on time. Margie's new thought process is shown in Figure 4.2.

Situation ⟶	Thought Process	▶ Behavior ⟶	Feelings
An engineer asks her to do a task she can't complete on time, if she is to finish what she is presently working on.	"It's important for me to say no, so I don't over-commit myself, and explain when I can real-istically get the job completed."	• Assertively states, "I'm working on a high-priority project now." • "I'm not able to get both this and your project com-pleted in the time you want." • "I could have it completed by about 11 a.m. tomor-row."	• Confidence • Improved self-esteem • Release of tension • Sense of power

FIGURE 4.2

Margie's Going Somewhere Cycle.

As you can see, listening to yourself is an important element of the listening process that is often neglected. People don't realize the power they have over their own behavior! By identifying nonproductive, inter-nal dialogue, we can reexamine the belief that caused a particular thought process. This self-examination allows us to learn when a certain thought process is useful and when it is self-defeating. By uncovering the belief that causes us to think negatively, we can formulate a modified version of that belief. This examination lets us get in touch with and hear exactly what is going on inside us that is causing us conflict and stress. The modified version will help us be in charge of ourselves more in the situations that formerly resulted in our going nowhere.

EXERCISE 4.1

As you were reading Margie's story, you might have become aware, by listening to yourself, of a Going Nowhere Cycle that you are experiencing. To increase your awareness of your internal thought process, analyze a situation in which you feel negatively about yourself or behave in manner you don't like.

Going Nowhere Cycle Awareness Check.

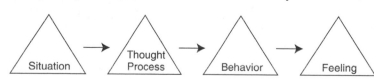

1. Think about that situation, then write a brief summary of what happens.

2. Now, focus on listening to the thought process you go through. Write down what you think.

3. Examine what you do as a result of this event and thought process. Note your behavior.

4. Now, note the feeling.

Carefully examine the words you used to describe what went on. Look for words such as *always, never, every, all the time, have to, should,* or *must.* Underline them. Such words don't allow choices or leeway in behavior. They force us to deal with ourselves in terms of either-or, this or that, should or should not.

Now, ask yourself, "What did I learn about myself that I want to modify or improve?" Note this information here.

After you have completed this portion of the exercise, use the same process to develop a Going Somewhere Cycle to counteract the Going Nowhere Cycle.

Going Somewhere Cycle.

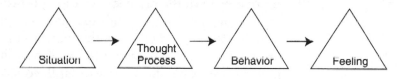

1. Again, describe the situation.

2. State a modified version of the old thought process, making sure you don't use the same negative terminology as you did in your Going Nowhere Cycle.

3. Imagine that his new thought process will result in effective and positive behavior.

4. Now, imagine how you will feel as you behave in this new manner.

To come full circle with this process, make certain to listen to your-self whenever you experience this situation in the future. If you start responding with the old negative thought process, tell yourself to Stop it. Replace the old dialogue with the new dialogue you have just developed. It might interest you to know that your brain can only think one thing at a time. Try it. See if you can think of two things simultaneously. You'll discover you can't. In other words, if you think positive thoughts, you don't think negative thoughts.

BELIEF SYSTEM PROCESS

When we listen to ourselves, we can increase our self-awareness and begin to understand why we behave the way we do. As you found by completing the Going Nowhere and Going Somewhere Cycles, one way to do this is to listen to your internal thought process. You learned that your thought processes influence the way you behave and feel. Chapter 2 described how our early socialization process influences our current listening habits and behaviors. We formulate beliefs early in life that later affect how we behave. These same beliefs also influence how we talk to ourselves. As long as our beliefs stay out of our awareness, we unconsciously set up roadblocks to personal and professional develop-ment. These unknowns about ourselves can result in nonproductive behavior, internal conflict, and feelings of frustration and defeat.

For example, when Margie delved into her negative thought process pertaining to "having to do everything for everybody," which resulted in her nonassertive and stressful behavior, she discovered she was behaving from a belief that said, "You have to do what you are told; you must not question authority." Her father, an engineer, would often say this to her when she questioned his reason for saying no to her. In other words, the message Margie's father frequently gave her was, "Do as you're told, and don't question me!" Margie interpreted this message to mean that her father's needs were more important than hers. Thus, she adapted to the belief as if it were a truth she shouldn't ever question.

Whenever something similar happened, she would automatically operate from this old belief that resulted in the negative thought process, that is, "I have to do everything for everybody."

Figure 4.3 shows Margie's Going Nowhere Cycle and the belief she was operating with.

Belief ⟶	Thought Process ⟶	Behavior ⟶	Feelings
"I have to do what I am told. I must not question authority."	"I have to do everything for everybody. I can't say no."	• Passivity • Overcommitment of herself • Tension, irritability	• Resentment • Irritation • Frustration • Pressure

FIGURE 4.3
Belief that led to Margie's Going Nowhere Cycle.

Frank's case is another example of beliefs formulated in early childhood.

As a child, Frank was taught by his parents not to talk when adults were around. If he did speak up, his father glared at him and his mother put her forefinger to her mouth as a signal for him to be quiet. Later, he was scolded for talking without permission.

Frank became aware of his parents' behavior during self-examination. Then he understood why he was having difficulty speaking up around authority figures. Whenever he wanted to express an idea or disagree with individuals who had more authority than he, he would clam up.

When he started to examine more fully the dynamics of what was happening, he discovered that he made mental pictures of his parents whenever his boss or another authority figure talked to him. He felt the old childhood fear and it temporarily immobilized him.

He discovered that, along with the internal imagery, he believed speaking up to authority figures showed disrespect. This belief led to a negative thought process and an internal imagery that left him feeling powerless and fearful.

Figure 4.4 shows Frank's Going Nowhere Cycle and the belief he was operating from.

Belief ⟶	Thought Process ⟶	Behavior ⟶	Feelings
Speaking up to authority figures shows disrespect.	• I can't express my ideas to those with authority. • I have to be quiet or I'll get into trouble.	• Passive • A yes-person • A follower • Waits to be told what to do	• Fear • Frustration • Anxiety • Tension

FIGURE 4.4
Belief that led to Frank's Going Nowhere Cycle.

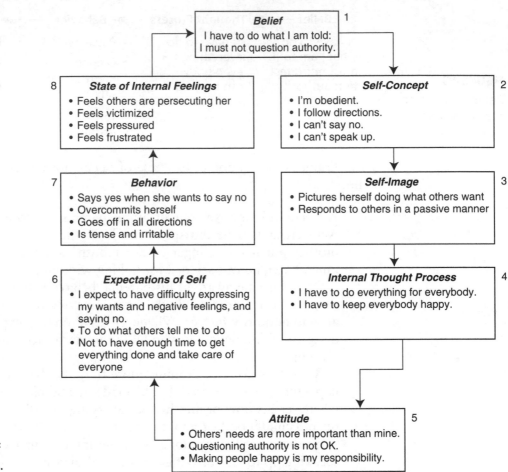

FIGURE 4.5

Margie's Belief
System Process.

Another dynamic of the preceding process is how the state of our feelings influences the way we act them out. Since we all have our own way of associating our behavior with the same state of feeling, the same feelings can be expressed in a variety of ways. Just because a person feels a certain way, it doesn't necessarily follow that he or she will behave the same way as someone else experiencing the same thing. As illustrated, Frank, when fearful, becomes immobilized. Margie, on the other hand, is motivated to get the work done. Fear of not pleasing others pushes her to work harder and longer.

Another common example is how anger is expressed. Some people let everybody within hearing distance know about it; others withdraw and become quiet. Although they may have the same internal state of anger, they behave differently when expressing that internal state.

Let's take a moment to examine what has been discussed so far by looking at Figure 4.5, which shows Margie's belief system charted out in a diagram.

As you were examining Margie's chart, the process probably became clearer to you. People seem to understand their behavior better when they actually see the process on paper. It helps them to get in touch with how the behavior evolves.

Notice that Margie's belief affected her self-concept, which then caused her to label herself. This labeling led her to behave in ways that reinforced her beliefs. Thus, she created the stressful situations on the job that she was blaming others for.

Her belief, self-concept, and self-image set the stage for her internal thought process, an internal verbalization that was often stated to others as well as to herself. This thought process resulted in an attitude that then influenced her to have certain expectations of herself. Margie created her experiences through these expectations. Therefore, she saw and felt what she expected to see and feel. Her world became a picture of her expectations: overcommitment, saying yes when she wanted to say no, and feelings of persecution and frustration.

Now that you've had some practice in analyzing how this process works, complete the following self-awareness exercise.

EXERCISE 4.2	**Belief System Process**

Take a moment to think of a belief you have about yourself. Like Margie, plot your belief system's process here.

1. State a belief you have about yourself.

2. Examine how that belief influences your self-concept. What affirmations of yourself might you say are a result of this belief?

3. Now, what images of yourself do you have? Describe the pictures here.

4. In response to this belief, your self-concept, and your self-image, what do you say to yourself?

5. Examine how the factors of the internal dialogue, the self-image, and the self-concept influence your attitude.

6. Explore what your expectations are as a result of the preceding information.

7. Now examine the kinds of behavior you get into. How do you behave?

8. What do you feel as a result of this behavior?

Action Plan

1. What did you find out about yourself?

2. Develop an action plan to modify or improve what you found out about yourself.

LANGUAGE BARRIERS

Negative Affirmations Expressed Internally

So far, you have seen how beliefs affect the self-concept and the internal thought processes that in turn affect behavior and feelings. You have learned that listening to yourself can help you become more aware of the things you say to yourself that influence how you behave and feel. Another phenomenon of this process is how negative beliefs lead to negative affirmations of yourself. Thus, it is important to pay attention to the internal affirmation that reflects the belief, "I can't listen effectively." This negative belief about the ability to be a skilled listener could lead to the following negative, internal affirmations:

"I can't understand . . ."
"I can't pay attention . . ."
"I always lose track of what people say . . ."

This "self-talk" could reinforce failure. It is an internal process of "Yes, but . . .," that goes like this:

"I should listen skillfully. Yeah, but I can't understand."
"I really ought to, because I'd feel better about myself. Yeah, but I can't pay attention, and anyway, I always lose track of what people say."

This "Yes, but" is a way to stay stuck behaviorally or to go in circles; a habit that inhibits personal effectiveness. This phenomenon is a reflection of the Going Nowhere Cycle.

The preceding example of the Going Nowhere Cycle would look something like the diagram in Figure 4.6.

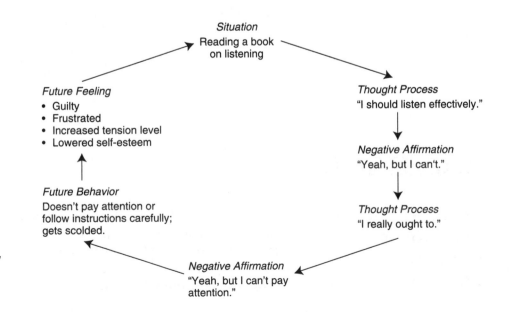

FIGURE 4.6
The "Yes, But . . ."
Going Nowhere
Cycle.

Negative Affirmations Expressed Externally

Your beliefs about yourself affect how you talk to others. Whenever we talk about ourselves to another person, we confirm how we see ourselves and how we feel about ourselves. Such phrases as the following would reveal much about the person saying them:

> "I'm not good at working with people."
> "Who, me? Maybe others can make a lot of money, but I'm not that lucky."
> "So . . . I'm not getting promoted as quickly as I should, but that's how it is, and there's nothing I can do about it."

Listening to how we affirm ourselves to others can be a big step toward changing old habits and perceptions of self. Nonlistening leads to nonawareness. Thus, we live our lives from an automatic, reactive mode, rather than a pro-action, choice mode.

The first chapter discussed areas of ourselves that we conceal from ourselves and other areas that are unknown. Psychologist Abraham Maslow referred to this phenomenon when he wrote

> . . . these portions of ourselves that we reject or repress do not go out of existence. They do not die, but rather go underground. Whatever effects these underground portions of our human nature have . . . tend to be unnoticed by ourselves or else felt to be as if they were not a part of us, e.g., "I don't know what made me say such a thing," "don't know what came over me."[8]

The value of listening to the way we talk to others and ourselves lies in the probability of learning about ourselves and developing our own potential.

"I Always"

Another language barrier to listen for, one that often leads to self-defeating behavior, is "I always." First of all, the word *always* puts an absolute to behavior: no leeway. *Always* leads a person to believe that a particular behavior happens every single time; no other behavior is possible. Other words with a similar effect are *never, all the time,* and *every time.*

Keith, a supervisor for a large bank, couldn't figure out why he felt depressed and often a victim. He referred to himself as a person who "always gets upset when I can't get cooperation out of my employees. . . . I always get anxious when I want to speak up at my department meetings. . . . I always feel let down after I handle a situation wrong." For Keith, and perhaps others, the idea of *always* makes things a lot easier. If something has always happened, we figure it's always going to happen. So, there isn't much point in attempting to do something about it: "That's the way it is, there's nothing I can do about it!"

For many people, the overuse of "I always" interferes with taking the initiative, being creative, and realizing and living out their full potential. It can lead to lowered self-esteem and lack of confidence.

The use of *always* results in looking at one's behavior in general, nonspecific terms. This kind of thinking usually leaves out the positive, successful behavior the individual does. Paying attention to "I always" self-references, and then replacing "I always" with more specific terms, can move one into being more positive about one's behavior.

For example, take the "I always" examples mentioned previously and replace them with positive, specific terms to illustrate the difference.

1. "I always get upset when I can't get cooperation from my employees."

   Changed Version:

   "I get upset when I don't get the cooperation I expect from Joe and Denise in getting their project done on time. I wonder if a different approach would be more effective?"

2. "I always get anxious when I want to speak up at my department meetings."

   Changed Version:

   "I sometimes become anxious at department meetings when I want to say something and I'm not sure how I want to say it. It probably would be useful to think things through, even jot notes down, before I speak at these meetings."

3. "I always feel let down after I handle a situation wrong."

   Changed Version:

   "I often feel let down when I don't handle a situation the way I would have liked. Perhaps I need some skill building in handling conflict."

EXERCISE 4.3

Take a few minutes to examine the difference between the "I always" statements and the changed versions.

1. List the differences here:

2. What have you learned that you could use in improving your effectiveness?

You might have listed some of the following differences:

1. The "I always" is part of a Going Nowhere Cycle.

2. "I always" is probably predicated on a negative belief.

3. Using the "I always" could lead to negative feelings.

4. The changed version is part of a Going Somewhere Cycle.

5. It is predicated on a positive belief that I can do things well.

6. Using the changed version could lead to problem solving and a positive feeling.

Labeling

Another dynamic of language barriers is "labeling." Individuals may experience the same physical feeling, but put different labels on what they are experiencing. What one person might label *anger,* another might label *anxiety,* another *hurt,* and so on. Listening to how we label our feelings is important in self-awareness.

It is important to listen to the language we use to label our behavior. Negative labeling—"I'm stupid," "I think too slowly to keep up," or "I never do anything right, I can't do that; it's too hard," leads to negative behavior, as we saw with Margie and Frank. It is a behavior modification method people use on themselves, resulting in the Going Nowhere Cycle and perpetuating failure. By replacing the negative language with positive reinforcements, we can get into the Going Somewhere Cycle, which perpetuates self-respect and success.

EXERCISE 4.4

To be more aware of the degree to which you use such statements, put an X on the continuum that indicates where you think you are in relation to that behavioral statement.

1. I sure got a lot done today.

say often	say sometimes	say once in a while	don't say

2. I still have two assignments to do. I never get everything done when I'm supposed to.

say often	say sometimes	say once in a while	don't say

3. I didn't do this job as well as it could have been done. Who could help me do it better?

say often	say sometimes	say once in a while	don't say

4. I botched it up again. I'm always doing dumb things.

say often	say sometimes	say once in a while	don't say

5. I didn't think that all the way through. What could I do next time so that I don't repeat this mistake?

say often	say sometimes	say once in a while	don't say

6. I never do anything right. If I weren't so stupid, I wouldn't have made this mistake.

say often	say sometimes	say once in a while	don't say

7. I don't understand why the manager is talking to me this way. What would be the most appropriate response?

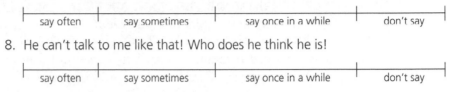

| say often | say sometimes | say once in a while | don't say |

8. He can't talk to me like that! Who does he think he is!

| say often | say sometimes | say once in a while | don't say |

9. Add any other positive or negative statements you hear yourself saying. Note them in the space below.

Now, examine your answers and identify those statements which you want to stop saying to yourself. Whenever you hear yourself say the negative statements, say to yourself, "Stop—that's no longer true. What's now true for me is _____
(positive statement)." Change the negative statement to a positive one. For instance, if you identified number 8 as something you say to yourself, you could change it to "I wonder why he talks to me like that. Perhaps I need to examine my behavior to find out what I do that influences him to talk to me that way." This type of exploration will keep you out of judgment and able to respond from level 1 and the OK–OK attitude. In addition, it helps you move into solving the situation rather than getting into blame and negative energy.

Identify those positive statements you want to repeat more often. Put those positive statements you want to repeat more often on 3 × 5 cards so that you can carry them with you. Whenever you have a free moment, take your cards out and repeat the statements our loud or to yourself. That way, you can begin to use positive behavior modification for your own professional development.

HABITS

Part of the socialization process is incorporating into your personality the behaviors and habits of your role models—most often, your parents and other significant people. These significant people often demanded overtly or implied through silence that we should follow their examples. Often, these examples didn't fit our natural or preferred way of doing things.

This programming results in the formation of habits. We are not born with habits—they are learned. Habits become a routine way of behaving and feeling. Repetition! Habits are a systematized set of feelings or actions resulting from old adaptations, often developed as a response to a childhood stimulus, long since forgotten, that now exists only in the brain. Yet unknowingly, we continue to unconsciously act out and feel the old responses to that past stimulus, and in so doing, we behave in old ways that are often inappropriate to the present situation.

One approach to modifying habits is not to focus attention on what someone else is saying and doing wrong, but rather on how you are experiencing their behavior. When you focus your attention on your response to the other's behavior, you can become more aware of your habitual responses to people and situations. This kind of focusing includes listening to the words you and the other person use that cause either strife or mutual cooperation.

This type of focusing can increase your effectiveness. When we are successful in our dealings with others, we view ourselves as confident and worthwhile. Thus, we will tend to imagine that others, in general, view us positively. However, if we have a negative self-concept and low self-esteem, we tend to imagine that others view us negatively or unfavorably.

What is striking about this phenomenon is that, in either case, we are not necessarily dealing with how others actually view us. What we are dealing with is our perception of how others view us. It is often a result of our inability to separate external reality from internal experience; i.e., we label what is going on with someone else based on our experience of the event, rather than the facts at hand. Information that we have been acquiring from our environment throughout our life has affected the formation of our beliefs. Once we have a mental image of ourselves and say, "I can't pay attention," we begin to feel we can't do it, excluding all other possibilities.

To maintain a positive self-concept, it is important to keep listening to yourself. Actively listening to how you use internal negative statements to interfere with your becoming an effective listener can be an important step to improved listening. Being aware of how you label your behavior negatively, judging yourself strictly, and using negative reinforcement statements can assist you in finding out what internal thought process you want to change.

People have the opportunity to do something constructive about their behavior that causes them difficulty when they observe themselves from a nonjudgmental, positive-thinking mode. The following are a few prescriptions that can help you deal with those negative statements and behaviors that cause you problems. It is an approach to handling yourself positively that will increase self-worth.

PRESCRIPTIONS

1. Approach mistakes as learning opportunities.

2. If you are unsure about the best way to solve a problem, think it through before actually doing it. This gives you a cognitive, trial-and-error run-through of the problem

3. You can use either supportive or suppressive language. Following are examples of both to provide a comparison.

Supportive language is when you:	Suppressive language is when you:
a. Tell yourself that you have done well (in specific terms): • "I work well under pressure."	a. Tell yourself what you have done poorly (in nonspecific terms). • "I don't do anything right."
b. Point out successes (in specific terms): • "I like the way I get things done in an organized way."	b. Reprimand yourself for failures: • "I shouldn't make mistakes, and I'm stupid for doing so." • "I'm always goofing up."
c. Deal with accomplishments: • "Next time, I'll get that project done on time with careful planning."	c. Deal with personal qualities: • "I goofed again. I'll never be fast enough to get this project done on time. I'm always so slow."
d. Positive reinforcement: • "I did that in record time." • "I'm getting better at doing that."	d. Self-criticism: • "I should have done it better." • "I'll never get better doing that."

Supportive language is when you:	Suppressive language is when you:
e. Examine the situation as an observer, and accept what you have done. Then ask: • "How could I have done it so I don't make that mistake again?" • "How could I do it next time that would get better results?" • "Where could I have gone to get the correct information?"	e. Quickly judge, criticize, and label yourself negatively. • "I'm sure stupid." • "I can't do anything right." • "I wish I could do it better, but I can't think well under pressure."
f. Believe that positive reinforcement is important to self-esteem: • "It is OK to give myself credit for what I do."	f. Have a bias about positive reinforcement. "If I praise myself, I will become immodest. Praise will get the better of me."

Keep in mind that both types of language can be reinforcing. The suppressing language can be as reinforcing as the supportive, but in a negative way.

I have found that supportive language works best because it leads to successful behavior and reinforces positive self-esteem. When we use suppressing language, it might get us started, but we don't feel good about ourselves. However, the tendency is to continue using the suppressing language and not move into the positive mode. Thus, we would get the task done, but we wouldn't feel good about ourselves. When people use negative reinforcement, rather than being internally motivated, they often feel that outside forces are driving them to behave in certain ways. People who use supportive reinforcement consistently feel that they have control over their lives. They most often find a positive reason to get unpleasant tasks completed. Their focus is on what would be useful to do, rather than what's wrong.

Using supportive language will keep us working at those things that are successful and that we want to continue. Using this kind of language will also help eliminate inappropriate behavior.

It is important to look at things we don't do well from the standpoint of learning and improving. When we are not making mistakes, we often don't take the time to evaluate our performance. Applying supportive reinforcement is one of the ways people can keep themselves out of the drama triangle. Often, the suppressing mode results in feeling victimized.

4. Practice using supportive language out loud when no one is around. That way it will be easier to say positive things about yourself to others when the occasion arises.

5. Evaluate yourself realistically. People often set unattainable goals of perfection for themselves. If you are constantly judging yourself against some unrealistic goal, you are bound to perceive most of your efforts as failures. Your evaluations must be accurate and real.

   a. Inaccurately evaluating what has been done. A person looks at a complete project and says, "I know I failed in doing it right." In fact, it was done correctly.

   b. Accurately appraising what has been done, but giving an unrealistic condition to it. A typist accurately estimates getting a typing project done with very few errors, then interprets the finished project as a failure when the prediction was not reached, or if someone else did it perfectly.

6. Set realistic goals. Often the goal operates as the standard against which we evaluate ourselves. If goals are unrealistic or unreasonable, we are, in a sense, adopting an unrealistic standard of evaluation. Then we evaluate our performance by how well we achieve the goal we set. It is beneficial to set short-range, achievable goals, goals that allow for positive self-reinforcement and reinforcement from others.

7. Frequently, we are dissatisfied with our judgments of self because we evaluate our choices as though we were choosing between perfect and anything else. Appropriate decision making is not a choice between one absolute good and one absolute bad. One difficulty with making value judgments is that individuals frequently are placed in the position of making choices between two conflicting right things or between two things that are less then ideal. When this happens, our feelings of worth result in constant dissatisfaction with our own judgments. Dissatisfaction is appropriate. However, feelings of unworthiness and a generalization of this dissatisfaction to the self-concept can lead to low self-esteem.

EXERCISE 4.5	**Self-Knowledge**

To get better acquainted with yourself, take 15 to 20 minutes each day, in a quiet place, to:

1. Reflect upon yourself, observe how you are interacting with others, and what your relationships with others are like.

2. Examine your beliefs and how they affect your behavior.

3. Explore and write out your purpose, your career plans, your goals.

SUMMARY

This chapter stresses the value of listening to yourself by being aware of your beliefs, your internal thought processes, the many ways in which you use language to talk about yourself, your habits, and your self-concept. These are avenues you can use for your professional development.

Listening to ourselves enables us to sift through the many things we experience, so that we can choose those things most valuable to us. Listening effectively to ourselves rests in our attitude, which includes being comfortable with ourselves. When we can observe who we are, critically, without undermining our self-worth, we can take credit for our accomplishments. A positive and accepting attitude allows us to be aware of those things that we like best about ourselves. That, in turn, will help us reshape those things we like least. It is easier to change behavior when we come from a positive position.

A listening attitude of enlightened self-interest allows us to learn many things of value about ourselves and those around us. Understanding that whoever you are is OK, is paramount to accepting yourself as you are.

SELF-TEST

1. What is the difference between the Going Nowhere Cycle and the Going Somewhere Cycle?

2. Identity two language barriers.

3. What is the value of listening to yourself?

4. What is the difference between supportive and suppressive language?

ANSWERS

1. The difference between the two cycles is:
   - The Going Nowhere Cycle leads to self-defeating behavior. We continue to be stuck in behaviors that result in failure, negative feelings, and life not working.
   - The Going Somewhere Cycle helps us be successful, have a sense of self-worth and a feeling of confidence, and know that we are in charge of what we do and who we are.
2. Language barriers are:
   - Negative affirmations thought internally and/or expressed externally
   - "I always" and "I never"
   - Labeling negatively who we are ("I'm stupid")
   - "I should, have to, must, am supposed to"
   - Suppressive language—"I can't, I can't do anything right."
3. Values of listening to yourself:
   - Becoming aware of how you limit your abilities by how you talk to yourself.
   - Changing negative internal dialogue to positive self-talk.
   - Beginning to learn who you are. This self-awareness is the first step along your path to reaching your potential.
   - Allowing yourself to find out what beliefs you have that interfere with being successful. Discovering what these beliefs are by listening to yourself will help you stop repeating self-defeating behavior.
4. Supportive language allows you to be your own best friend; suppressive language influences you to treat yourself like your own worst enemy.

   Suppressive language lowers self-esteem, supportive language usually increases it.

   People using supportive language are in charge of their lives; people using suppressive language feel out of control and often have one crisis after another.

5 Making Listening Work for You

The only things worth learning are the things you learn after you know it all.

Harry Truman

Previous chapters have discussed many factors that influence listening habits and patterns, patterns that affect which listening level you use most often. One crucial time to be an effective listener (level 1 listening) is when another person is discussing a problem with you that he or she feels strongly about. This chapter discusses this type of situation and has exercises to improve your listening habits.

The way you listen to and respond to others will strongly influence how they will respond back to you and how they will feel about your response, such as wanting to continue talking, feeling turned off or understood, tense or relaxed, etc. The interaction would look something like the diagram shown in Figure 5.1.

(Stimulus) S 1: The other person making a statement about his or her problem,

(Response) R 1: Your response to other's problem, which becomes a stimulus for:

R 2: The other's response to your response.

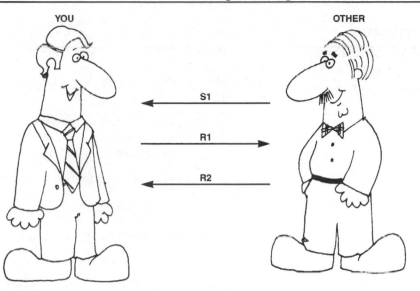

FIGURE 5.1
The communication
interaction.

LISTENING ASSESSMENT

The following listening assessment provides the opportunity to examine your listening behavior patterns in such situations. Keep in mind that this is a work-related situation as you complete the assessment. When you finish the assessment, score yourself.

LISTENING ASSESSMENT EXERCISE*

Put a check by the letter that best describes your first response to the person in the situation who is expressing a problem. You are not looking for the right response or how you would like to respond, but how you *would*, indeed, respond to people in these situations.

1. "I don't know what I'm going to do. I'm making all kinds of mistakes, and I know my supervisor is unhappy with me. He's already yelled at me two times."

   _____ a. "Why do you make mistakes?"

   _____ b. "You should tell your supervisor how you feel."

   _____ c. "You seem worried that you are making mistakes and that your supervisor is upset with you."

   _____ d. "Your supervisor probably has good reason to yell at you. You should do something about making so many mistakes."

---

*A modified version of the listening instrument authored by Madelyn Burley-Allen, published by Training House, Princeton, N.J., 1981.

2. "The company policy is supposed to be to hire from within the company. And now I find out that this new guy is coming in to replace my boss. I had my eye on that job; I've been working hard for it. I know I could prove myself if I had a chance. Well, if that's what they think of me, I know when I'm not wanted."

_____ a. "It can be discouraging when the company seems to have forgotten about you by hiring outside the company, especially when you put a lot of hard work into your job."

_____ b. "Your qualifications probably don't compare with those of the new man."

_____ c. "You ought to make sure they know your views and let them know your interest in advancement."

_____ d. "Did they discuss it with you at all?"

3. "My supervisor often makes mistakes and has me handle the situation for him. It ends up that he avoids confronting the issue directly. To add insult to injury, he says to me, `It's your fault, you should watch for those mistakes,' but they are really his errors . . . ."

_____ a. "I wouldn't let anybody treat me that way. Are you sure it's not your fault?"

_____ b. "It sounds like you're caught in a double bind; you resent being treated this way and are wondering what you can do about it."

_____ c. "What kinds of mistakes does he ask you to cover up?"

_____ d. "You should quit that job and find one where you're treated fairly."

4. "It happens every time the manager appears in my department. He just takes over as if I weren't there. When he sees something he doesn't like, he tells the employee what to do and how to do it. The employees get confused, I get upset, and finally he leaves. I'm responsible to him, so what can I do?"

_____ a. "You should discuss your problems with your boss."

_____ b. "When did this start to happen?"

_____ c. "The boss must be the boss, I suppose, and we all have to learn to live with it."

_____ d. "It upsets you that your manager takes over and is not sure how to handle the situation."

5. "It's happened again! I was describing an office problem to my boss and she starts staring out the window. She doesn't seem to be really listening to me because she has to ask me to repeat things. I feel she's superficially giving me the time to state my problems, but she ends up sidestepping the issue."

 ____ a. "You should stop talking when you feel she's not listening to you. That way she'll start paying attention to you."

 ____ b. "You can't expect her to listen to every problem you have; anyway, you should learn to solve your own problems."

 ____ c. "What kind of problems do you talk to her about?"

 ____ d. "I can see this is frustrating to you."

6. "I think I'm doing all right, but I don't know where I stand. I'm not sure what my boss expects of me, and he doesn't tell me how I'm doing. I'm trying my best, but I wonder who else knows that. I wish I knew where I stood."

 ____ a. "Has your boss ever given you any indication of what he thinks of your work?"

 ____ b. "You should discuss it with him."

 ____ c. "Perhaps others are also in the same position, so you shouldn't let it bother you."

 ____ d. "Not knowing if you're satisfying your boss leaves you feeling unsure, and you'd like to know just what he expects from you."

7. "As long as I've got a goal ahead, I'll keep striving for it. I'm determined to advance; hard work never bothered me. I know it won't be easy, and I'll probably have to climb over a few people to get my way. This is important to me; I want to be somebody, and I will be!"

 ____ a. "You shouldn't have to climb over people to get what you want."

 ____ b. "Getting ahead is very important in your life, even if it means hard work, and it won't be easy."

 ____ c. "What in particular do you want to achieve?"

 ____ d. "You should take some management classes to help you advance."

8. "I'm really tired of this. I come in in the morning, and already I've got twice as much work as I can do. And then they say, 'This is a rush,' or 'Hurry up with that.' I've got so many people asking me to do things that I just can't keep up, and it bothers me. I like my boss, and my work is interesting, but I could use a vacation."

_____ a. "With so many people asking you to do things, it's difficult for you to get everything done, and the pressure gets you down."

_____ b. "Are all these requests from other people part of your job?"

_____ c. "You seem to have too much work. You ought to talk it over with your boss."

_____ d. "You probably are overworked because you're not organized."

9. "I work like mad to get rush projects completed! What's my reward for getting them out? Nothing! No thanks, no nothing. In fact, most of the time the so-called rush projects are sitting on people's desks unattended for days."

_____ a. "How often does this happen?"

_____ b. "You ought to tell them you don't like being treated this way."

_____ c. "Sounds like you feel others are taking unfair advantage of you."

_____ d. "You shouldn't get so angry."

10. "He used to be one of the guys until he was promoted. Now he's not my friend anymore. I don't mind being told about my mistakes, but he doesn't have to do it in front of my co-workers. Whenever I get the chance, he's going to get his!"

_____ a. "To be told about your mistakes in front of co-workers is embarrassing, especially by a supervisor you once worked with."

_____ b. "If you didn't make so many mistakes, your boss would not have to tell you about them."

_____ c. "You should talk it over with a few people who knew him before and then go talk to him about this situation."

_____ d. "How often does he do this?"

On the next page, circle the listening responses you checked.

Empathetic Response:

A nonjudgmental response that captures the essential theme and/or feeling expressed, a potential for building rapport and mutual understanding.

1-c,   2-a,   3-b,   4-d,   5-d,   6-d,   7-b,   8-a,   9-c,   10-a.

Advice Response:

A response that offers advice, tells the talker what to do or what not to do, solves the problem, or does the thinking for the talker.

1-b,   2-c,   3-d,   4-a,   5-a,   6-b,   7-d,   8-c,   9-b,   10-c.

Asking Question Response:

A response that asks for additional information to get a clear understanding before responding. Used to excess, the talker may feel "grilled."

1-a,   2-d,   3-c,   4-b,   5-c,   6-a,   7-c,   8-b,   9-a,   10-d.

Critical Response:

A response that expresses a form of criticism resulting from a natural tendency to judge, approve, or disapprove of a message received.

1-d,   2-b,   3-a,   4-c,   5-b,   6-c,   7-a,   8-d,   9-d,   10-b.

I.   Examine your listening response pattern.

     1. The response I use most often is

     2. The next response I use most often is

     3. The next response I use most often is

     4. The response I use least is

**LISTENING
ASSESSMENT
EXERCISE**
(continued)

II. 1. What does this listening response pattern tell you about yourself?

2. What do you want to maintain?

3. What do you want to modify?

4. What is one thing you can do to put this modification into effect?

Hopefully, by completing this exercise, you discovered specific listening patterns that are either hindering or enhancing your relationships with people you work with.

THE LISTENING RESPONSE SYSTEM ANALYSIS

This instrument has been completed by about 7,000 people attending my seminars over the course of 14 years. Total team scores for each category are as follows:

1. 18,718 Recommendation Response

2. 13,465 Asking for Information Response

3. 19,164 Empathetic Response

4. 7,791 Critical Response

Often, the people who had a high score in empathetic listening had read a book or two about listening and had attended other training seminars that included this listening skill response. A very small percentage of those people with a high score in this category, maybe 5 to 10 percent, said the response came naturally or they learned to use it based on experience. Seems we do, indeed, socialize people to give advice, ask questions, and be critical, none of which is truly listening at level 1. Being aware of those four responses will help you listen more easily at level 1, which is empathetic listening. To make listening work for you, do the following:

1. Avoid being critical and judgmental. This type of listening usually increases the emotional level of the talker, or else he or she feels turned off and chooses not to continue the conversation. The critical response pattern is often experienced as persecution by others, along with the feeling that they are not "OK." It seems to influence the other person to move to level 3 or 2 in response to what was said to them.

2. Listen to the underlying meaning of what was said, empathetically and nonjudgmentally, to improve your ability to listen at level 1. This style of listening helps build understanding, trust, and rapport, allowing the other person to feel that he or she can talk without being criticized or judged. It helps talkers solve their own problems. When people have a better understanding of their own behavior, they can make sense out of what is happening. Keep in mind that you don't have to agree with what the person is saying to be an empathetic listener, you only have to empathize with the talker's feelings and what he or she may be experiencing.

3. The timing for asking questions is very important. It is usually best to hold your questions until you have listened empathetically at level 1. Sometimes an empathetic response must be made two or three times before the talker's emotional level has lessened to the level where he or she can think objectively and listen at level 1. By helping the person bring his emotional level down, the listener provides an effective function for the talker. People solve problems more effectively if they can be logical and analytical. Emotions interfere with objectivity.

4. Refrain from solving the talker's problem or doing the person's thinking for him or her. This listening style can lead to the rescuer listening mode that was discussed in Chapter 3. People feel more self-confident when they can solve their own problems and think them out themselves. Although giving advice can make the listener feel

needed and important, it is done at the expense of the talker's personal and professional development. We have a myth in our society that when someone has a problem, we're supposed to solve it. I think our function is to listen nonjudgmentally, allowing the person the freedom to work the problem out himself.

An example of this system being used was Janet, the supervisor, responding to Jim's lost report problem in Chapter 1. Janet helped Jim reduce his emotional level by listening empathetically and aided his remembering of what he did with his report. She held back criticism by not saying, "Can't you do anything right?" She also did not jump in and rescue Jim by looking for the report herself. Janet asked questions like, "What do you do then?" and, "When did you last remember having the report?" Notice that she didn't use "why" questions. In such situations, "why" is often heard as a criticism. As part of the socialization process, children often hear "Why did you do that?" "Why didn't you do that?" The question has an underlying message that says "You'd *better* come up with the *right* answer or you'll be in *trouble!*" It is often heard as a personal attack.

To handle this kind of criticism, a child responds by being defensive, or justifies his behavior with a "Yes, but ____." Often the "Why did you" leads to going around in circles. People don't always know why they do things, they just do them, often without any thought to their motivation. "Why" also leads to a defensive or justifying "Because." For example,

> S: "Why did you do that?"
> E: "Because I didn't know."
> S: "Why didn't you know?"
> E: "Because no one told me."
> S: "Why didn't you ask someone?"
> E: "I don't know."

In dialogue, the conversation goes around in circles, and feelings of frustration are felt by both parties.

What, how, when, where, or *who* questions more often work toward finding a solution. Instead of "Why did you," you could say, "What were your reasons for doing the assignment this way?"; How could you have done it differently to avoid this error?"; or, "Where could you have gone to follow the proper procedure?" For example:

S: "How could you have done this task so this error wouldn't have happened?"

E: "I wasn't certain the procedure I used was correct, but I went ahead anyway because no one was around to assist me."

S: "I see. I can understand your reasons for going ahead; you wanted to get the job done."

E: "Yes, that's right."

S: "I'd like to go over the procedure with you now to check your understanding. Show me how you will follow the procedure the next time you do it."

Graphically, the procedure would look like the diagram in Figure 5.2. (In response to someone who is telling you about a problem they are having).

EXERCISE 5.1

This exercise will give you an opportunity to practice identifying the four responses. Examine the situations and note in the space provided which response category (empathetic recommendation, informative, critical) you think fits that response.

Situation I

"Oh, brother! Did a woman in our department get a promotion by buttering the higher-ups! That promotion should have been mine. I think I was more qualified than she. She doesn't need the money half as much as I do; what woman does?"

Response Category	Responses
a. _____	"It seems to me that you haven't done your job as well as you think you have, or you would have received the promotion yourself."
b. _____	"It's distressing to have someone get a promotion you were banking on, especially when you feel you were more qualified."
c. _____	"Has this happened to you before?"
d. _____	"If I were you, I'd tell my manager how angry I was feeling."

- Don't be critical.
- Don't ask questions at this time.
- Don't ask *why* questions.

- Being critical can increase the level of emotions or turn them off.
- Do listen empathetically to bring the emotional level down, build understanding and rapport.
- Summarize what the talker said.
- Now—ask *what, when, how, who, where* questions.
- Facilitate problem solving by . . .
  - being a resource person.
  - relating facts, ideas, and other relevant information.
- Do give positive feedback for thinking their problem through and deciding on a solution.
- If appropriate, schedule a follow-up meeting.

TALKER'S EMOTIONAL LEVEL IS HIGH

Talker with a problem.

FIGURE 5.2
Listening response system.

EXERCISE 5.1
(continued)

Situation II

"I don't know what I'm going to do. My boss keeps asking me to stay overtime to get letters out for the next day. I can't say anything because he's my boss. I'd sure like to tell him a thing or two, but I just can't risk it."

Response Category	Responses
a. _____	"Sounds like you feel you're being taken advantage of and want to find a way to confront your boss about his behavior."
b. _____	"If I were you, I'd discuss it with him. You should tell him how you feel."
c. _____	"If you didn't act like a doormat, you would have stood up to him by now."
d. _____	"Has your boss always treated you this way?"

Compare your answers with those that follow:

Situation I	Situation II
a. Critical	a. Empathetic
b. Empathetic	b. Recommendation
c. Asking questions	c. Critical
d. Advice	d. More Information

EXERCISE 5.2

Now that you've had an opportunity to identify the four responses, this exercise will give you practice on coming up with your own responses that fit each of the four categories.

Situation I

"If only I had enough money, I would jump at the opportunity; I'm sure I could make a go of that business. All a person needs is a little vision, some common sense, and the courage to try it, and I've got all that. I just don't have the money to do it. That's life, I guess."

Empathetic Response:

EXERCISE 5.2
(continued)

Recommendation Response:

More Information Response:

Critical Response:

Situation II

"It all boils down to the fact that I'm in the wrong job. I've hesitated leaving for a long time because I spent four years in college preparing myself for this type of work. Now I think I would be happier if I leave this job behind and enter this other field—even though I'll be starting at the bottom of the ladder."

Empathetic Response:

Recommendation Response:

More Information Response:

Critical Response:

Compare your responses with those that follow:

Situation I

Empathetic: "It's discouraging not to have the money you need to get into a business you feel you'd make a success of."

Recommendation: "What you should do is discuss it with a bank manager."

More Information: "What kind of business is this?"

Critical: "Are you sure you could make a go of a business of your own?"

Situation II

Empathetic: "To change fields after spending four years attending college is a big decision—one that's not easy for you to make."

Recommendation: "You really should stay with the job you have, since you don't know what you're getting into if you change jobs."

More Information: "What is it that appeals to you in this other field?"

Critical: "Do you think you should give up four years just like that?"

ATTRIBUTES OF AN EFFECTIVE LISTENER

Another way to make listening work is to be aware of the attributes of an effective listener. Tests conducted at the University of Minnesota identified several common attributes of effective listeners. Good listeners looked for an area of interest in the speaker's message; they viewed it as an opportunity to gather new and useful information. Effective listeners were aware of their personal biases and were better able to avoid making automatic judgments about the speaker and to avoid being influenced by emotion-charged words. They also tended to listen to ideas, rather than specific facts in a message. These people used extra thought-time to anticipate the speaker's next statement, to mentally summarize the message, to question or evaluate the message, or to consciously notice nonverbal cues.

Another research study done by the author identified the following characteristics for ideal listeners:

- They keep an open, curious mind.

- They listen for new ideas everywhere, integrating what they listen to with what they already know.

- They are aware and thus listen to others with their total being.

- They listen from the heart to help stay nonjudgmental.

- Being this aware, they are not willing to blindly follow the crowd.

- They maintain conscious perspective on what is occurring, rather than remaining unconscious and missing important details.

- They look for ideas, organization, and new ways of doing things, and listen to the essence of things.

- Knowing that no two people listen in the same way, they stay mentally alert by outlining, clarifying, approving, and adding illustrations of their own.

- They are introspective and have the capacity and desire to critically examine, understand, and attempt to transform some of their values, attitudes, and relationships within themselves and others.

- They focus their attention on the talker's ideas while listening with feeling and intuition.

METHODS TO IMPROVE YOUR LISTENING SKILL

Chapter 1 cited Dr. Ralph Nichol's studies, which show that we devote 40 percent of our day to listening, yet, his tests revealed, listen at only 25 percent efficiency. With training, our listening skill can be improved so that we listen at level 1 more often. Some things you can do to improve your skill as a listener are:

1. *Search for Something You Can Use; Find Areas of Common Interest.*

   If you adopt a positive attitude toward a subject, you will usually find something in any talk that will broaden your knowledge. Dry though a talk may be, it will generally contain an idea that is worthwhile to you, now or later. Sorting out elements of personal value is one area of effective listening. What is being said that I can use? What's in it for me? How does this relate to what I already know? What action could I take?

2. *Take the Initiative.*

   Find out what the talker knows. Look at the talker and concentrate on what has been said. Go all the way in making the communication two-way. Ignore the person's delivery and personality if they distract you. Reach for the idea that is being conveyed. Stimulate the talker with your attentiveness and expressions of interest. Show interest by the use of noncommittal acknowledgments such as: "Oh, I see," "How about that," "mm-hmmm, interesting," "Really, you did," and so on.

3. *Work at Listening.*

   Efficient listening takes energy. Practice makes it easier. If the subject is announced in advance, prepare for it by reading, by discussing it, or by thinking it over briefly, establishing your own point of view. Then listen actively and energetically.

4. *Focus Your Attention on Ideas.*

   Listen for the speaker's central ideas. In some cases, you will recognize the conventional toastmaster method of building a speech, from the opening introduction of the subject, the transitions from point to point as the theme evolves, the word pictures and examples, and the concluding summary or call for action. Pick out the ideas as they are presented, sort the facts from principles, the ideas from examples, and the evidence from opinion.

5. *Make Meaningful Notes.*

   You can improve your ability to learn and remember by making a brief record of the speaker's main points. Review your notes later on to determine what you can put to use, and whether you agree or disagree with the speaker's thesis. Efficient note-taking requires practice in selecting the right method of notes for each occasion, but whatever the method, make the notes brief, easy to interpret, and easy to review. Depending on the nature of the talk, practice making an outline, mental or written, or picking out the key words, phrases, or ideas. Stay flexible; many speakers do not follow a precise outline.

6. *Resist External Distractions.*

   Where possible, resist distractions. Sit where you can see and hear without being distracted—concentrate on concentrating. When you concentrate on concentrating, you make it possible to be aware of noises without being distracted by them.

7. *Hold Your Rebuttal; Watch Out for Hot Buttons.*

Don't let emotion-laden words throw you. Begin to recognize certain words that affect you to the point where you stop listening and start forming a rebuttal. One way to deal with this is to quickly analyze the reasons those words stir you, then resume listening, withholding any judgment until you fully comprehend what point the speaker is making. Another method is to jot down major rebuttal points as questions; do this briefly, not at length. Both methods can help clear your mind so that you can return to listening with an open mind.

8. *Keep an Open Mind: Ask Questions to Clarify for Understanding.*

Quick and heated disagreement with the speaker's main points or arguments can cause a psychological deaf spot. Keep your mind open. Give the talker *more* rather than less attention. Search for the full kernel of the theme. Stay out of the judgmental framework by not judging what the person says as "wrong." Clarify meaning by restating, in your own words, what you thought was said.

9. *Capitalize on Thought Speed; Summarize.*

The core of effective listening is to develop the utmost concentration on the immediate listening situation. Concentrate on what the talker says. Summarize in your head what the talker said. Decide how well he is supporting his points and how you would have supported them. Mentally review, after each point is covered, the progress of the theme; contrast and compare, identify the speaker's evidence.

10. *Practice Regularly.*

Get experience and practice in listening and note-taking by listening to difficult or unfamiliar material that challenges your mental capacities. Every club meeting could present many opportunities for practice. Regular practice will work wonders for you. Efficient listening takes effort, but it is one of the easiest ways known to acquire ideas and information you can use.

11. *Analyze What Is Being Said Nonverbally.*

Be patient and sensitive to the talker's feelings. Ask yourself why the talker said what he or she did, and what she or he meant? Listen between the lines for hidden meanings. What is the person saying nonverbally?

12. *Evaluate and Be Critical of Content, Not the Speaker's Delivery.*

It's important to discriminate if the talker is stating facts or assumptions. Decide how well he or she is supporting the main points and how you would have supported them. Hear the talker out before judging. Getting the talker's message is more important than his or her appearance. Don't let the talker's poor voice, mannerisms, personality, or appearance get in the way of the message. Recognize that most people are not very skilled at getting their message across.

These methods can be used to improve your listening habits. Most people discover that they can overcome poor listening habits by systematically incorporating these twelve tools into their listening behavior.

For example, Cliff, a personnel manager, found he improved his skill as an interviewer significantly by applying one of these 12 techniques. He became aware of his level 2 listening during interviews because of his misuse of thought speed. Instead of capitalizing on thought speed, as described in method 9, he thought of what he was going to say next, or listened only to the first part of what a person was saying. While the interviewee was going on to the second part of his discussion, Cliff was busy formulating a question inside his head in relation to what the interviewee said first. Thus, Cliff often asked a question that the interviewee had already covered in the first part of his discussion.

Cliff gradually overcame this disruptive habit by listening at level 1, which allowed him to be aware of how he formulated questions inside his head while an interviewee was still conveying information Cliff needed. He learned to wait to ask a question, summarize what the interviewee said, and then ask his question if he didn't get the information he wanted. By doing so, he reduced the time he spent in each interview while obtaining more relevant information.

Concentration and Retention

The methods of improving your listening skill will increase the time you spend at level 1, along with your ability to concentrate and retain information. Information we listen to at level 1 will be more readily remembered. Thus, it appears that better listening promotes better memory.

One way to start developing this skill is to *process* the information you are listening to. Processing means associating what is said with something familiar to you, repeating the information internally or out loud, or summarizing what the person has said. What a person does with time lag will strongly influence the amount of information listened to and ultimately remembered.

Often, this time lag works to our disadvantage. Instead of using the methods mentioned, we are likely to think of other things—mental tangents flashing through our brain—while the speaker is talking. Daydreaming is a primary alternative to listening.

A process that helps me listen and remember more effectively is to picture in my mind what the speaker is saying. For instance, I'm working with an associate, Arlene, who calls me on the phone to suggest that she could pick up a mailing project from my office on Monday morning to start working on while I'm out of town. She tells me she will need certain material to complete the job. Picturing her in action not only helps me listen better, but also ensures that I remember the conversation.

Another useful tool is to talk over what you've heard. Talking about what was said with another person helps to clarify your thinking and increases what you remember.

Since most people listen at 25 percent efficiency, spending 75 percent of their time at level 2 and/or 3, it is important to keep the following points in mind when talking.

1. When you are speaking and making only one point, people probably need to hear it only once.

2. If you make two or three points, listeners will more than likely need to have it repeated. They won't remember your points without repetition.

3. If you are making four to five points, you'll need to repeat the information along with another sensory tool, such as having the listener write it down, summarizing what was said out loud, using pictures or graphs to reinforce what was said, or having the listener walk through what you are talking about.

4. Beyond six points, you'll need to use two or more of the above sensory tools.

By using these various approaches, you help yourself and the other person listen at level 1. Another method for doing this is the empathetic listening mode.

Empathetic Listening Mode: Level 1 Listening

Most supervisors' results are accomplished through person-to-person communication. By its nature, managing involves people. A major function of supervisors or managers is to facilitate better understanding among the people they work with. It is largely by these people contacts that managers and supervisors influence and motivate those they supervise. Skillful listening develops the information, insight, and understanding needed to deal with people effectively and to successfully manage an organization.

Many people have found the empathetic approach to listening to be a powerful tool for improving their people skills. Some payoffs have been increased sales, improved ability to sell ideas to management, improved ability to handle emotional people, more effective interviews, and improved working relationships.

By listening actively, a person demonstrates interest in what the talker is saying. This sets into motion a supportive chain in which the talker feels more accepted and can be more open. This, in turn, allows the talker to give more valid information that enables the listener to ask relevant questions. The active, empathetic listening mode can be a big step in making listening work for you.

Carl, a manager for a large manufacturing company, had this to say about the power of empathetic listing at level 1:

Improving my listening skills has been a major reason why I have advanced in my career and become so successful at working with people. My increased ability to listen at level 1 has had several positive results and improved personal relationships. My manner of managing others is different from what it used to be. At performance appraisal time, my effective listening encourages the employee to discuss with me the negative things that are going on. By doing this we are able to solve the problems, thus reducing the amount of negative energy expended by the employee. I have consciously worked at listening, and I find the negative interactions I used to have at performance appraisals are almost eliminated. I actively listen to what's not being said and to what's being said.

In the past, when I had a different person to deal with, I was quick to judge and be critical, which moved me into listening levels 2 and 3. I found myself forming rebuttals and thinking they were "not OK." Now I'm aware of when I start to get into that mental process and stop myself. I then concentrate on what's being communicated beyond the words, and force myself into the "OK–OK" mode by asking myself internally, "What's going on that I'm being negative about?"; "Why am I reacting this way?"; or, "What could I do to listen nonjudgmentally?"

What's interesting is that my improved listening skills have influenced changes in other parts of my behavior. Before I knew about the levels of listening, I used to think I understood what was said to me. I would misunderstand assignments given to me, and when I was corrected for doing them accurately, I would blame the other person for my negative feelings. I now perform my job more efficiently, and the amount of work I complete is increased. Needless to say, I feel better at the end of the day.

I used to have a difficult time dealing with a key manager in the corporate headquarters. But when I made a point of listening beyond his gruff manner and often critical facial expression, I discovered that I had let these mannerisms move me into the "I'm not OK" and "he's not OK" listening mode. Forcing myself not to judge him quickly didn't come easy, but I stayed with it. At the beginning, I could only find a couple of ways to react to him positively. However, he was affected by my effort and my new behavior. After what seemed to be forever, I was able to discuss my feelings with him. The final result is that working with him is now bearable, and it's getting better all the time.

Like Carl, others have found that this active, empathetic listening approach eases understanding of what the other person really means. Keep two important ideas in mind when interacting with others: (1) People prefer talking to listening, and (2) the listener actually controls the conversation. To listen effectively and be in control of what is being said, check your understanding regularly by summarizing what the other has said. Then, wait for feedback—either confirmation that your understanding is correct or clarification of what the speaker intended.

This method can be used advantageously when the talker is emotionally upset, when you want to listen objectively in problem solving and conflict situations, and when you are being criticized unjustly or justly. Active listening can assist you to keep your cool, remain objective, and be empathetic to the other person's point of view.

Guidelines for Empathetic Listening

1. Be attentive. Create a positive atmosphere through nonverbal behavior. When you are alert, attentive, nondistracted, and have eye contact, the other person feels important and more positive.

2. Be interested in the other's needs. Remember, you are to listen with understanding.

3. Listen from the "OK-OK" attitude.
   a. Be a sounding board; allow the talker to bounce ideas and feelings off you while you assume a nonjudgmental, noncriticizing manner.
   b. Don't ask a lot of questions. Remember, questions can come across as if the person is being "grilled."
   c. Act like a mirror: Reflect back what you think the other is feeling and/or saying to you.
   d. Because they discount the person's feelings, don't use stock phrases such as:
      • "Oh! It's not that bad."
      • "You'll feel better tomorrow."
      • "It will blow over; don't be so upset."
      • "You shouldn't feel that way; it's only a small matter."
      • "You're making a mountain out of a molehill."

4. Don't let the other person "hook you." This can happen when you get angry, hurt, or upset, allow yourself to become involved in an argument, jump to conclusions, or pass judgment on the other person.

5. Other ways to indicate you are listening:
   a. Encouraging, noncommittal acknowledgment; brief expressions:
   "Hum."
   "Uh-huh."
   "I see."
   "Right."
   "Oh!"
   "Interesting."

   b. Nonverbal acknowledgments:
   Head-nodding
   Facial expression (matching what the talker is saying)
   Body expression or movement that is relaxed and open
   Eye contact
   Touching
   c. Door-openers. Invitations to say more, such as:
   "Tell me about it."
   "I'd like to hear what you're thinking."
   "Would you like to talk about it?"
   "Let's discuss it."
   "Sounds like you've got some ideas or feelings about this."
   "I'd be interested in what you have to say."

6. Ground Rules
   a. Don't interrupt.
   b. Don't take the subject off in another direction.
   c. Don't get into internal distractions.
   d. Don't interrogate.
   e. Don't preach.
   f. Don't give advice.
   g. Do reflect back to the talker what you observe and how you believe the talker feels.

The preceding guidelines provide a detailed description of the active listening mode, an overview of this listening approach. The chart shown in Figure 5.3 treats the information more specifically and provides examples of listening techniques.

People often find it hard to identify what they are feeling, let alone what others are feeling. Although they have little difficulty recognizing behaviors, they are unable to identify the feeling experienced along with the behavior. You can help yourself to do this by using the "feeling-check" listening response. To use the feeling-check listening response, you need a list of feeling words at your disposal. See Figure 5.4.

Feeling-Check Listening Response

Often people have more trouble using the feeling-check response than the other responses. Many people have been socialized to believe that expressing negative feelings and even feeling them is "not OK." As a result, this is the hardest listening response mode to incorporate into their level 1 listening habits.

Listening Objective	Method	Listening Technique
I. *Clarifying Check*		
1. When you want to clarify, want facts, want to explore further, or to check assumptive meaning and understand	State a what, how, or when question. Then restate what you thought you heard.	1. "Is this the problem as you see it?" 2. "Will you clarify what you mean by . . . ?" 3. "What specifically do you mean by . . . ?" 4. "What I understand you to say is . . . . Is that right?"
II. *Accuracy Check*		
1. To check your listening accuracy and encourage further discussion. 2. To let the person know you grasp the facts	Restate the person's basic ideas, emphasizing the facts.	1. "As I understand it, the problem is . . . (restatement). Am I hearing you correctly? 2. "What I think you said was . . . ."
III. *Feeling Check*		
1. To show you are listening and understanding 2. To reduce anxiety, anger, or other negative feelings 3. To let the person know you understand how he or she feels	Reflect the person's feelings. Paraphrase in your own words what the talker said. Match the talker's depth of meaning, light or serious. Ensure accurate communication of feelings by matching the talker's meaning.	1. "You feel that you didn't get the proper treatment." 2. "It was unjust as you perceived it." 3. "It's annoying to have this happen to you." 4. "It seems to me that you got turned off when your boss talked to you in that angry manner." 5. "I sense that you like doing the job but are not sure how to go about it."

FIGURE 5.3

Ways the listener can be in control: establishing and maintaining the flow of communication.

FIGURE 5.3
(continued)

Listening Objective	Method	Listening Technique
IV. *Summarizing Check*		
1. To focus the discussion and to lead to a new level of discussion	Restate, reflect, and summarize major ideas and feelings.	1. "These are the key elements of the problem."
2. To focus on main points and to offer a springboard for further consideration		2. "Let's see now, we've examined these factors."
3. To pull important ideas or facts together		3. "These seem to be key ideas you express."
4. To review progress		4. "To summarize, the main points as I heard them are . . . ."
V. *Noncommittal Acknowledgment*		
1. To stay neutral and show you are interested	Don't agree or disagree. Use noncommittal words with a positive tone of voice.	1. "I see . . ."
		2. "Uh-huh . . ."
2. To encourage; to keep a person talking	Express noncommittal acknowledgment.	3. "Mm-hmm . . ."
		4. "I get the idea . . ." "I understand." Silence during the pause.
VI. *Door Opener*		
Acknowledge the problem.	Show willingness to discuss the problem.	1. "Tell me about it."
		2. "That does seem to present a problem."

The model shown in Figure 5.5 illustrates how this listening response works. The object of this listening response is to link the event with the speaker's feelings.

The talker's feelings may be expressed nonverbally in the voice tone, facial expression, posture, and/or gestures. After the feelings have been heard or sensed by the listener, the listener puts both the feeling and the event or facts into a sentence. The "you feel" component of the feeling-check response acknowledges the credibility of the talker and demonstrates the listener's acceptance of the talker as a person as well.

The example in Figure 5.5 shows the feeling being expressed before the event or facts. However, the event could be stated first. For instance,

Mild	Anger	Elation	Depression	Fear
	annoyed	glad	unsure	uneasy
	bothered	pleased	confused	tense
	bugged	amused	bored	concerned
	peeved	contented	resigned	anxious
	irritated	comfortable	disappointed	apprehensive
		surprised	discontented	worried
		relieved	apathetic	
		confident	hurt	

Moderate	Anger	Elation	Depression	Fear
	disgusted	cheerful	discouraged	alarmed
	harassed	delighted	drained	shook
	resentful	happy	distressed	threatened
	mad	up	down	afraid
	put upon	elated	unhappy	scared
	set up	great	burdened	frightened
		hopeful	sad	
		eager		
		anticipating		

Intense	Anger	Elation	Depression	Fear
	angry	joyful	miserable	panicky
	contemptuous	excited	ashamed	overwhelmed
	hostile	enthusiastic	crushed	petrified
	hot	turned on	humiliated	terrified
	burned	moved	hopeless	terror-stricken
	furious	enthralled	despairing	
		free	anguished	
		proud		
		fulfilled		
		fascinated		
		titillated		
		engrossing		
		absorbing		

FIGURE 5.4
Feeling words.

FIGURE 5.5

Listener's summarization model.

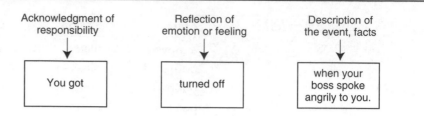

you could say, "When your boss speaks angrily to you, you get turned off." There is probably some additional value in using a changing or random order to avoid the mechanical or stilted quality of the response.

Some alternate ways of starting the "you feel" part of the listening response method are:

"It sounds as if you're . . ."
"You'd like . . ."
"You seem . . ."
"It appears to me . . ."
"What I'm perceiving is . . ."
"My hunch is . . ."
"I sense that . . ."
"What I heard you say is . . ."
"What I see going on is . . ."
"If I understand, you feel . . ."

Any approach can become mechanical and undermine the objective of demonstrating genuine, empathetic acceptance and understanding of the talker's message. It's important when applying any technique to do so with the intent of improving the interaction and responding to the talker's needs.

Some examples of the active, empathetic listening response were given in the listening assessment at the beginning of the chapter. Review these responses to better understand them.

EXERCISE 5.3

This exercise will give you practice in using the feeling-check listening response. After reading the talker's statement, write in the active, empathetic response you think best reflects what he or she is feeling.

1. Talker

"I'm expecting my boss to firmly assert our position on the performance review procedure at the meeting today. I hope he doesn't come on too strong. He can become emotional when he feels strongly about something he really believes in."

Listening-Feeling Check

Acknowledgment of responsibility	Reflection of feeling	Description of event or facts

2. Talker

"I know not getting work out will get me in trouble, but I really want to get even with my supervisor for not appreciating all the work I've done by working during my lunch hours and breaks."

Listening-Feeling Check

Acknowledgment of responsibility	Reflection of feeling	Description of event or facts

3. Talker

"I have a terrible time saying no when I don't have time to get something done that a co-worker is asking me to do. I end up doing what they want at the expense of not getting my own work done."

Listening-Feeling Check

Acknowledgment of responsibility	Reflection of feeling	Description of event or facts

EXERCISE 5.3
(continued)

4. Talker

"My department's budget got cut way back."

Listening-Feeling Check

Acknowledgment of responsibility	Reflection of feeling	Description of event or facts

Responses:

1. "You sound *concerned* that your boss might put his foot in his mouth at the meeting."
2. "You feel *resentful* that your efforts are going unnoticed."
3. "Seems to me, you feel *frustrated* by not being able to get your own work done because you don't say no when you want to."
4. "You're *worried* about how you are going to handle the department finances with the budget being cut back so much."

EXERCISE 5.4

Now that you've had some practice at responding to situations using the listening-check response, turn to page 129 and study the chart titled, "Ways the listener can be in control." Using that chart as a guide, improve the following dialogue between Jim and Sarah. In the dialogue, Sarah's responses are those a person might make who is listening from level 2 or 3. In the spaces given, make any changes to Sarah's responses that you think would show better active, empathetic listening on Sarah's part. You may also change what Jim might say in response to your modified version of Sarah's response.

Jim: "We've got a real problem, Sarah."
Sarah: "Now what?"

Jim: "We can't go any further with the Johnson sales campaign because the word-processing machine broke down."
Sarah: "Not again! Well . . . did you call the repair service?"

Jim: "No, it wouldn't do much good because it takes them at least a day for a repair person to get here."

Sarah: "How do you know that's the case this time? You'd better call them anyway."

Jim: "If you say so . . . although I don't think it's going to do us any good."

Sarah: "Well, do it anyway. Why don't you send the material to a word-processing firm to get it done?"

Jim: "I thought of that already. But that's not good either. The only one that can do this kind of job is all the way across town."

Sarah: "You don't have any choice. You'd better take it to the firm across town now!"

Compare your changes to the ones stated below.

Jim: "We've got a real problem, Sarah."

Sarah: "Mm-hmm, tell me about it."

Jim: "We can't go further with the Johnson sales campaign because the word-processing machine broke down."

Sarah: "That does present a problem. What have you done so far?"

Jim: "I've thought about calling the repair service, but it wouldn't do much good because it takes them at least a day to get someone over here. The other option I thought of was to take it to another word-processing firm. The trouble is that the only one who can do this kind of job is all the way across town."

Sarah: "I see. Sounds like taking the job to the firm across town would be the fastest way to go."

Jim: "Yeah, I guess so. I hate to go all the way across town just to get one job done."

Sarah: "You feel frustrated that you have to take time out of your busy schedule to do this."

Jim: "Yeah. It would probably be best to delegate it to Dave, since he's working on something that doesn't need to be finished until next week."

Sarah: "Sounds like that would work. Let me know how it works out."

Jim: "I will, thanks."

Incorporating the empathetic approach into the way you listen to others can provide many benefits. For example, a group of nursing service administrators working for a hospital in Oklahoma organized a project that would use this listening approach at group meetings.[9] The groups were set up to define problem areas without increasing discontent among staff members.

Using the active listening format, the service administrators acted as receivers of information while striving to understand what the individual staff member was feeling. The service administrators then put this information into their own words and repeated it for verification. This was the only feedback—nothing more, nothing less. As the receivers, they did not send any messages of their own, such as evaluation, analysis, or questions.

The empathetic listening approach allowed the individual senders of the messages to say more and develop their own thoughts about problem areas. It also encouraged the senders to develop personal insight and begin problem solving.

The use of active listening techniques assisted the nursing administration in a variety of ways:

1. It permitted ventilation of troublesome feelings.

2. The staff became less uncomfortable with their negative feelings as they perceived that the administration was willing to listen openly and with acceptance.

3. It promoted a more comfortable relationship between the administration and staff.

4. Staff members were guided from merely talking about problems to posing alternative solutions.

5. Within ensuing discussions, the staff appeared to be more receptive to the administrator's thoughts and ideas on potential solutions. It also appeared that the staff was more willing to try the proposed suggestions.

This process enables the speaker to work out his or her own problems. The responsibility of solving the problem remains with him or her. New insights, new ways of doing things, new attitudes, and new understandings of self are frequently the long-term effects of this approach.

By giving verbal feedback of what was said or done, along with a guess at the feeling behind the spoken words, the listener communicates acceptance. Since this acceptance is given without criticism and judgment, the talker feels that he or she has been heard and understood, which increases trusting relationships. Because the talker has an opportunity to vent his or her feelings, the feeling level is lowered, and he or she often experiences relief.

SUMMARY

In this chapter, you found out what your listening response pattern looked like by completing the listening assessment. The listening response analysis provided you with a format that could be used when applying the four response categories in difficult situations. These categories are empathetic, recommendation, asking for more information, and critical.

The attributes for ideal listening were covered, as well as the 12 methods of improving your listening skills. You found that you can increase level 1 listening by improved concentration and retention. This can be done by processing what the speaker is saying through associations, by visualizing, and by talking over what was said with someone else.

For empathetic listening, the guidelines were covered that will assist you in putting the empathetic listening approach into practice. This listening mode allows the speaker's feelings to be validated. By giving verbal feedback of what was said or done, along with a guess at the feelings behind the spoken words, the listener communicates acceptance. Since this acceptance is given without criticism and judgment, the talker feels heard and understood; this increases trustful relationships. Because the speaker has an opportunity to vent his or her feelings, this feeling level is lowered, and he or she often feels relieved.

SELF-TEST

1. Name the four listening response categories.

2. Which of these listening responses are people programmed in their childhood to use?

3. Name four attributes of an effective listener.

4. Twelve methods to improve your listening were discussed. Name three of them.

5. Figure 5.3 included six listening objectives. Name two of them.

ANSWERS

1. Empathetic, advice, asking questions, and critical.
2. Advice, asking questions, and critical.
3. Does not judge

   Is understanding and empathetic

   Listens from the heart

   Listens at level 1

   Focuses on the talker's nonverbal behavior in order to respond effectively to the talk.

   Check pages 119–120 for additional attributes.
4. See pages 120–123 to check your answers.
5. Clarifying, accuracy, feeling, summarizing, noncommittal acknowledgment, and door opener.

6 Getting Others to Listen to You

Two men were walking along a crowded sidewalk in a downtown business area. Suddenly one exclaimed, "Listen to the lovely sound of that cricket!" But the other could not hear. He asked his companion how he could detect the sound of a cricket amidst the din of people and traffic. The first man, who was a zoologist, had trained himself to listen to the voices of nature, but he did not explain. He simply took a coin out of his pocket and dropped it on the sidewalk, whereupon a dozen people began to look about them. "We hear," he said, "what we listen for."

Bhagwan Shree Rajneesh,
The Discipline of Transcendence

The previous chapters have emphasized the role of the listener and the various habits people develop that interfere with listening. The focus has been on the listener and the characteristics of listening at the three levels.

Another vital ingredient of effective listening is being aware of the power you have of getting others to listen to you. It seems that, as we listen well to a talker, he or she becomes aware of it and develops a subconscious desire to listen to us when our turn comes.

If we want to be effective in our dealings with others, it is important to know the kinds of things we do that influence others to listen to us. Often heard complaints are phrases like these: "I'd like to help one of my co-workers, but he won't listen to anything I say." Or, "I want to help, but people get defensive when I give advice." Knowing what behavior turns people off can be significant in improving your ability to influence others positively. You, as a talker, can do various things to motivate people to listen to you. This can be achieved by your choice of words, nonverbal behavior, tone of voice, attitude, how you ask questions, and how you give feedback.

NONVERBALS: THEIR EFFECT ON THE SPEAKER

First consider how nonverbal behavior can motivate a listener positively or negatively. Chapters 2 and 3 dealt with this subject from the listener's perspective. This time the focus is on the talker. What nonverbal behavior can you, as a talker, use to get the other person to listen to you when it is your turn to talk?

EXERCISE 6.1

To sharpen your awareness of this dimension of the listening process, take a moment to examine the nonverbal behaviors listed here. Imagine yourself in the talker's role.

Put a P (for positive) by the behaviors that you, as a talker, could use to influence the listener to listen to you. Put an N (for negative) by those behaviors you think would not get the listener to listen to you.

1. _____ Raising an eyebrow

2. _____ Smiling

3. _____ Nodding your head

4. _____ Sitting forward in the chair

5. _____ Remaining silent

6. _____ Frowning

7. _____ Looking away from the listener

8. _____ Rolling your eyes

9. _____ Opening and relaxing your body posture

10. _____ Touching

11. _____ Being attentive

12. _____ Putting your hands on top of your head

13. _____ Not moving

14. _____ Behaving restlessly

15. ____ Hanging your head down

16. ____ Having eye contact

17. ____ Sighing

18. ____ Squinting your eyes

19. ____ Withdrawing

20. ____ Looking delighted

21. ____ Scowling

22. ____ Reaching out

23. ____ Slumping in your chair

24. ____ Folding your arms across your chest

25. ____ Tilting your head down

26. ____ Narrowing your eyes

27. ____ Arching your neck forward

28. ____ Looking at the listener sideways

29. ____ Having a critical facial expression

30. ____ Looking straight at the listener

31. ____ Drumming your fingers

32. ____ Shrugging your shoulders

33. ____ Puffing your cheeks

34. ____ Pulling back the corners of your mouth

35. ____ Swishing your foot

36. ____ Shaking your finger

Certain behaviors are interpreted the same way by most people, and other behaviors are interpreted differently. It is generally agreed that behaviors 1, 6, 7, 8, 12, 14, 15, 17, 18, 19, 21, 23, 24, 25, 26, 28, 29, 31, 32, 33, 34, 35, and 36 are interpreted as negative. The remainder are seen as positive.

As you were identifying these nonverbal behaviors as positive or negative, you might have had difficulty determining if the behavior was positive, negative, or both. How a nonverbal behavior is interpreted by the talker adds still another dimension to the dynamics of the situation.

For instance, "Hmm" can be said at least six different ways. Each conveys a different message. I'm sure you have had experiences in which someone said "Hmm" to you in a pleasing way, while someone else said it to you in a critical way. Just for fun, take a minute and say this expletive in various tones and emphases. You'll find it can be expressed in many ways that could be heard by the talker as encouraging or discouraging.

To add another dimension to this exercise, have someone you know identify the behaviors without showing that person your answers. Then, compare your answers. You will probably find that your answers are different in some instances.

Another example of nonverbal behavior that can have several interpretations is silence. It can be so cold that you shudder in response to it; it can be so warm that you are encouraged to continue and feel supported by it; or it can be a neutral message to continue talking.

Withdrawing may signify various behaviors such as avoidance, stopped listening, hearing at level 3, or listening at level 1. When we stop listening and withdraw within ourselves, our voluntary muscle activity ceases, the interval between eye blinks lengthens, and the eyes take on a staring, glaring look. This behavior interferes with the listener's ability to pay attention to what the talker is saying, since it is often an expression of anger or boredom. Often people experience high levels of discomfort when a talker assumes this behavior while they are listening.

Movement is another behavior that can motivate or distract the listener. A certain amount of movement by you, when it is your turn to listen, can indicate that you are, indeed, listening because listening means being stimulated and involved. A listener is engaged, attentive, and open; this involves some kind of movement. However, other kinds of movement by you, such as restlessness, impatient body movements, frequent shifts of weight from one foot to another, could be interpreted as negative—a sign of boredom or impatience. Nonmovement or no reaction often tells the listener that you have withdrawn into yourself or have moved into level 3 hearing. Brainwave tracings show a different pattern for the person who is listening from that of a person who is only hearing or who is momentarily withdrawing.

Certain behaviors by the talker are often perceived by the listener as being critical. While you were doing the previous exercise, you probably noticed that some of the behaviors you decided were negative felt critical to you; for example, raising an eyebrow, frowning, looking away from the talker, having a rigid body posture, scowling, folding your arms across your chest, or narrowing your eyes. People often respond to such critical behavior by reacting belligerently or apologetically toward the talker.

When you look judgmental and talk in an opinionated way that shows disapproval, the listener tends to work harder at what he or she will say when it's his or her turn to speak. The talker often tries to please you so that you will stop disapproving and start approving of what is being said. This criticism can influence the talker to become self-conscious, thus losing his or her train of thought, expressing him- or herself less clearly, or saying what he or she thinks you want to hear. This type of communication can have a great deal of negative control over the listener.

You can persuade or dissuade the other person from continuing along a particular line of thought. You can get others to listen to you, simply by the way you listen to them when it's their turn to speak. Whether or not you are aware of this ability to influence another person, you *can* influence a talker with your nonverbal behavior.

Bruce, a manager of a customer service group, gave this example to a seminar group I was conducting about the impact his nonverbal behavior had on his staff.

During our first session, I realized from the feedback I received from Tim that my nonverbal behavior needed to be modified. This confirmed my intuitive feelings that something was not going well with my staff. Since I was new on the job, whenever they came to me with a problem, while listening, I was busy thinking about how I should solve it. I didn't realize that I was frowning in a manner that seemed angry and critical. They would react defensively and would stop listening. When Tim told me that most of the time I frowned while doing a listening practice session, the light bulb went on.

The day after our session I discussed what I learned with my staff. Sure enough my frowning was an issue. I guess when you are 6 feet 4 inches and 190 pounds, a frown can have a real impact on people. My staff also told me I tended to fold my arms across my chest, which to them felt I was closing them off. Getting that honest feedback from Tim has already made a difference.

The important component in this story is Bruce's willingness to be open to Tim's feedback and then to act on it. We all can learn from Bruce's example. How many people do you know who go to seminar after seminar and don't change one bit? It takes real commitment and desire to grow and develop.

NONVERBAL LISTENING APPROACH

You can use nonverbal behaviors to your advantage so that you influence the listener positively. By responding to the listener in a motivating manner, you start a positive communication chain. It seems that good speaking and listening habits, as well as poor speaking and listening habits, are not only contagious—they are also self-perpetuating. It is most important to get started in the right direction.

By becoming more aware of your own speaking style, you can improve your ability to communicate with and understand colleagues, superiors, and other people you work with. You can actually use nonverbal behavior to help the listener communicate to you better when it is his or her turn to talk. This starts the positive communication chain that leads to better understanding, mutual agreement, breaking down of resistance, and minimizing distortion of what is being said.

In the previous list of nonverbal behaviors are several that can help you to get others to listen to you. The following is a suggested, nonverbal listening approach you can put into practice:

1. As a general rule, assume a "leveling posture." This involves looking straight at the listener, maintaining eye contact 60 percent of the time, and squaring the head and face so you achieve a level-headed, open, relaxed body posture, and a straightforward attitude. Keep in mind the characteristics of level 1 listening.

2. Be vocally attentive by using acknowledging words such as "I see," "Gee," and expletives like "Hmm," "Uh huh." People prefer vocal stroking to silence. The overall vocal tone used when expressing these expletives or acknowledging words is extremely important. As discussed earlier, they can be expressed with a positive or negative quality. (You might want to practice using a tape recorder to check out how they sound.)

3. Use positive movement by leaning forward, arching your neck forward, nodding your head in agreement, and, when appropriate, touching the speaker's arm.

4. Facial expressions have a tremendous effect on individuals. Smiling, looking interested, and other positive expressions have a powerful

motivating effect on the listener. Make sure you use them sincerely. People quickly recognize a false front.

5. Minimize the negative behaviors covered earlier—remember that critical listening and negative nonverbals can have a disruptive effect on people.

6. Use the active, empathetic listening style whenever appropriate to build rapport and trust.

ATTITUDE

Chapter 5 discussed in detail the characteristics of an active, empathetic listener. The last several pages have described how critical nonverbal behavior affects the listener negatively. It's interesting to compare the two styles in relationship to one's attitude, since the talker's attitude has a strong motivational effect on the listener. The two styles have some distinct differences:

ATTITUDINAL STYLES

Fault-Finding	Empathetic
1. Dominating position (rigid, frowning, etc.)	1. Leveling posture (open, relaxed, etc.)
2. Level 2 or 3 listening	2. Level 1 listening
3. Judgmental	3. Descriptive
4. Unaware	4. Aware
5. Superiority	5. Equality
6. Formulates rebuttals	6. Processes what it is said and checks for understanding
7. Opinionated	7. Thoughtful
8. Restrained	8. Spontaneous
9. Control oriented	9. Problem-solving oriented
10. "I'm OK—I'm not sure about you . . . yet."	10. "I'm OK—You're OK."

LISTENING ASSESSMENT EXERCISE

Most people find themselves somewhere in between these two styles. As a way to assess this for yourself, take a moment to examine your behavior by placing an X on the continuum that best states where you see yourself in relation to the fault-finding behavior and a 3 for the empathetic behaviors.

Attitudinal Style Assessment

1. Dominating position • Leveling posture

| almost never | someplace in between | most of the time |

2. Level 2 or 3 listening • Level 1 listening

| almost never | someplace in between | most of the time |

3. Judgmental • Descriptive

| almost never | someplace in between | most of the time |

4. Unaware • Aware

| almost never | someplace in between | most of the time |

5. Superiority • Equality

| almost never | someplace in between | most of the time |

6. Formulates rebuttals • Processes what is said and checks for understanding

| almost never | someplace in between | most of the time |

7. Opinionated • Thoughtful

| almost never | someplace in between | most of the time |

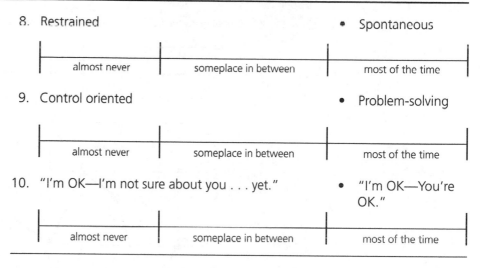

8. Restrained   • Spontaneous

|_____|_____|_____|
almost never   someplace in between   most of the time

9. Control oriented   • Problem-solving

|_____|_____|_____|
almost never   someplace in between   most of the time

10. "I'm OK—I'm not sure about you . . . yet."   • "I'm OK—You're OK."

|_____|_____|_____|
almost never   someplace in between   most of the time

EXERCISE 6.2

As a result of this assessment, you might have found behaviors that you might want to improve upon. People find it beneficial to develop an action plan for incorporating the behavior they want to use most often or for decreasing the use of the negative ones.

For instance, you might want to stop yourself from forming rebuttals while a person is talking and instead listen at level 1. The plan you would develop could look like this:

Improvement Action Plan

1. Every day I will work on stopping myself when I become aware of forming rebuttals while a person is talking.

2. I will do this for three weeks starting _____ (date) and ending _____ (date).

3. I will keep a graph of my progress to measure how well I am doing in reaching my goal. (See the sample graph shown in Figure 6.1.)

4. *Analysis:*

    a. When did I find it easiest to stop forming rebuttals?

        Hardest?

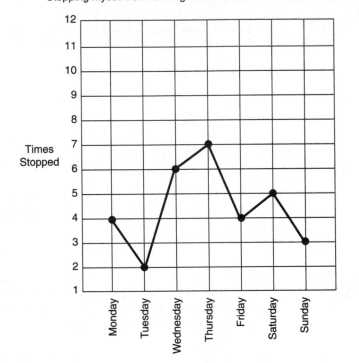

Stopping myself from forming rebuttals and instead listen at Level 1.

FIGURE 6.1

Example of an improvement graph.

EXERCISE 6.2
(continued)

b. With whom did I have the most difficult time stopping myself from forming rebuttals?

The easiest?

c. What similarities and differences are there between work and my personal life?

d. In examining the answers just given, has a pattern evolved? If so, what is it and what can I do about it?

5. A part of you doesn't like giving up an old habit. It's important to positively reinforce yourself for putting the time and energy into overcoming this old behavior. Rewarding yourself is essential to getting cooperation from that part of you that doesn't want to give it up. Here are some rewards people have used to motivate themselves.

   a. Take an extra half hour at lunch time (of course, with your boss's permission).

   b. Buy yourself a small gift that you usually wouldn't buy, like a bouquet of flowers, a ticket to a sports or musical event, or an extra special lunch or dinner.

   c. Give yourself some time alone.

   d. Take time to enjoy your favorite hobby.

   e. Take a half-day off to do nothing.

   f. Do something you've wanted to do but never had time for.

   g. Sleep late on Saturday.

   h. Brag to a friend or relative about how well you did.

   i. Pat yourself on the back for completing your agreement and sticking to it.

   j. Take $30 out of your savings account to buy something foolish.

With persistence, the old behavior will gradually diminish. After a while, you will find yourself listening more often at level 1 and forming rebuttals less often. Once this new behavior becomes a habit, you can move on to another contract and repeat the process.

WAYS THE TALKER CAN INFLUENCE LEVEL 1 LISTENING

People are often not aware of their listening habits and haven't been taught to listen or talk in ways that help the listener listen more effectively. The key to successful communication is whether or not our message has been understood and accepted by the listener in the same terms as we intended it. The following are guidelines for talkers to be more effective in getting others to listen to them.

GUIDELINES FOR TALKERS

- Know what you want to say
- Know as much about the listener as possible
- Gain favorable attention—be aware of your nonverbal behavior
- Secure understanding
- Aid retention
- Encourage feedback

Know What You Want to Say

It's important to have the objective of your message and your information clear in your mind. Being certain of what you want to say is an important first step in building a positive communication chain. It is difficult for the listener to understand information clearly if the talker conveys it in fuzzy terms. What often happens is that the listener puts fuzzy information together in a way that makes sense to him or her, often not realizing that it wasn't what the talker intended. Both individuals come away from the interaction thinking that understanding took place, which often leads to misunderstandings and arguments.

Know as Much about the Listener as Possible

It's natural to gather information, consciously or unconsciously, about the people we deal with. As we work with people day by day, we accumulate bits and pieces, and sometimes whole chunks, of information about them. Often, by reading another's nonverbal behavior, we can gather clues about their internal state that could assist in effectively interacting with them. Having an understanding of people makes it easier to handle their behavior.

For instance, it is helpful for the talker to know how much others can handle stress, criticism, or emotional situations when the need arises to confront them about something they have done inappropriately. The problem that often occurs is that this data gathering comes from assumptions rather than facts. The tendency is to make assumptions that may not be entirely true but make sense to us, and thus seem factual. When we interact with people on false assumptions, we can cause communication barriers. The more our understanding is based on facts we gather about others, the more effectively we will be able to deal with them and respond to them appropriately.

Sarah had this to say about this guideline:

I had to submit a report to my manager, who is very different than I am. I felt pretty good about how I had designed and written the report. What I wasn't feeling good about was my presentation of the material.

After we covered the six guidelines for talkers, I realized I was uncomfortable about the focus and emphasis of the introduction in terms of this manager's interest and values. I had written the introduction emphasizing what I valued, not what this manager valued.

I got together with a friend from another department who knew my manager well. We brainstormed what we thought were his values and interests in terms of my report. I incorporated this into my presentation introduction and in various sections in the report.

He responded favorably to my report and okayed the monies needed to implement it. I know if I hadn't incorporated his values and interests there could have been a good chance the report would have been rejected.

Sarah learned a critical lesson. We don't persuade people who have different interests then we do by talking about our own interests. Many people take for granted that people value what they value and lose out. Level 1 listeners listen to other people's needs, interests, and desires so that they can respond to them successfully.

Gain Favorable Attention

You can gain favorable attention by responding to the person using the empathetic style of listening, along with positive nonverbal behaviors. By doing so, you can help establish trust and confidence. People feel important when someone listens to them in this manner. Varying your vocal inflection and speed will help you hold the listener's attention. Anticipate the listener's interest in what you are going to say, then talk in terms of that interest. As was discussed in Chapter 3, people listen more readily to what interests them.

Secure Understanding

Each person is at a different level of understanding. When someone talks over a person's head, it can be taken as a put-down by the listener, and the talker is often labeled as "putting on airs." On the other hand, talking below a person's understanding can also be perceived as a putdown, because the listener feels "talked-down-to." Thus, it is important to use language appropriate to your audience. As often as possible, start with agreement. Simple, specific terms are less likely to be misunderstood. Present ideas one at a time or in small bits. Whenever possible, relate your suggestions to a previously successful experience.

Aid Retention

To help ensure retention, associate new ideas with those already familiar to the listener. Periodically summarize the items mentioned. If necessary, you or the listener can write down the main points. To make sure you have communicated clearly, ask the listener to restate what he or she thought was conveyed.

Many people complain that these suggestions take too much time. At the start they could, but eventually, they will probably help save time. For example, these methods have cut down on the misunderstandings between my secretary and me by about 40 percent. They have helped decrease misinterpretations, additions, deletions, and frustrations.

Encourage Feedback

People tend to overestimate their accuracy as listeners. The same is true about talkers; they overestimate the listener's accuracy, too.

Without feedback, we often think we have understood when in fact we haven't. To increase understanding, it is useful for the listener to ask questions about what's being said. The talker requires feedback to know that he is being understood.

To encourage feedback, ask for ideas and suggestions. Stop from time to time to ask questions, and allow the listener to respond to what is being said. If a person doesn't provide feedback, you have no idea whether or nor your message has been received as intended.

The ideal communication model is not linear, but circular.

a. It not only provides for passage of the message form the talker to the listener, it also allows for feedback from the listener.

b. This allows the speaker to amplify and adjust his message to the listener.

c. Without using feedback, it is difficult to create understanding.

This circular process would look like the diagram in Figure 6.2.

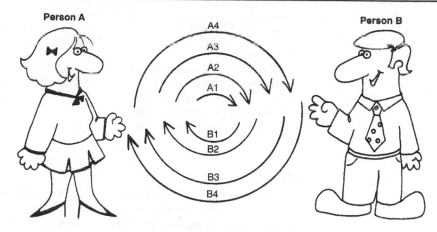

FIGURE 6.2
The circular communication model.

The Art of Asking Questions[10]

Encouraging feedback and securing understanding enables you to test your assumptions as well as the assumptions of the person you are interacting with. By so doing, you can minimize the chance of distortion and deletions. The following examples illustrate how asking questions can aid in this endeavor.

Situation	Sample Questions
Unfamiliar Phrases	
1. The talker has used an unfamiliar phrase.	"Could you elaborate on what you mean by "psychological barriers to listening"?
Encourage without Bias	
2. The talker is getting into sensitive areas and has stopped talking. You want to encourage without biasing.	"You say things started to fall apart when the customer became very angry."
Digressing	
3. The talker is digressing and is not telling you what you were waiting to hear.	"Perhaps I'm mistaken, but weren't you going to tell me about what you did that wasn't taken care of?"
Going in Circles	
4. The talker has been going in circles, saying the same things over and over. You want to move on.	"Let me summarize what I understood you to say. You said (a)_____ (b)_____ and (c)_____ Now, was there anything else affecting the problem?"

Situation	Sample Questions
Generalization	
5. The talker has not explicitly stated what you think is behind the words, so you employ the "risk technique" and state what you think is on his or her mind.	"Is this the situation: You feel that if I don't take care of this right now, I won't call you back?"
Clarification	
6. The talker has just said something that does not seem to agree with a statement made earlier. You want to clarify.	"I thought you said a few minutes ago that _____. Now I hear you saying _____. These two statements seem to be in conflict. Would you clarify?"
Checking Understanding	
7. The talker has stated an opinion, and you want to check your understanding.	"In your opinion, we have too many people taking their lunch at the same time, so the counter is not covered properly to give the best customer service. Is that right?"
Checking the Reason for Not Accepting Your Modification	
8. The talker won't accept a revision you have suggested, and you want to check the reason.	"I'm aware that we have handled employee grievances in the past in the way you've described. I'm wondering what it is about this one modification that makes it unacceptable to you?"
Obtaining Ideas	
9. You want to obtain the thoughts and ideas of the talker about something you or the talker said.	"I think this is how the flextime approach would affect the morale in the office. What are your thoughts about it?"
Drawing Out Reservations	
10. The listener has responded nonverbally, as though he or she is bothered by something you said. You want to draw out his or her reservations.	"Something seems to be bothering you about what I just said. Will you tell me what it is?"

Situation	Sample Questions
Obtaining Feedback	
11. You have stated some benefits of an idea and want feedback from the listener.	"How do you think these benefits will give us the results we are looking for?"
Focusing	
12. Several suggestions have been stated, and you want to focus attention on them.	"We've given several suggestions. Which one do you think will most likely provide us with the best solution?"
Clarifying Resistance	
13. The listener has disagreed with part of what you have said, and you want to clarify the resistance.	"You think the idea is basically a sound one, yet it seems to have flaws in it. What would you do to reduce these flaws?"
Checking for Specifics	
14. The listener has made a general statement about an issue you're discussing, and you want to talk in explicit terms.	"What specifically has been done that you think is wrong?"

People have found that using such questions helps them interact with others from the empathetic mode, which results in an increase of level 1 listening and the "OK–OK" listening style. Asking the appropriate question assists the talker in being less defensive and often leads to problem solving, rather than making people feel personally threatened. This kind of questioning has other advantages. It helps keep the conversation more objective and relevant to what is being said, it decreases the chances of the discussion going off on tangents to unrelated topics, and it helps the listener listen to what the talker is saying.

EXPRESSING FACTS VERSUS ASSUMPTIONS

When talking to others, it is important to keep your thinking straight. Personal impressions are not the same as facts and the actual events that have taken place. Assumptions obtained from observations often seem like facts. Getting into the habit of describing explicitly what you want to say will establish credibility, making it easier for the other person to listen to you and understand you more easily, and finally, follow what you are saying.

For example, a person might say, "I don't see any reason for hiring an outside firm to do our accounting. Their price would be outrageous; and even though they'd do a good job, I don't think it would be worth it."

This example is an opinion stated in general terms, based on the assumption that has not been clarified. When people talk in this manner, the listener often has the urge to formulate a mental rebuttal and often does. Now the conversation is no longer a discussion on the pros and cons of hiring an outside accounting firm, but rather an argument over

---

EXERCISE 6.3

Turn to pages 153–155. Which of the question categories could be used to clarify what the talker said in the preceding example? Note the question category and what you would say in the space following.

You might have used the following question categories and said something like this.

1.   2 – *Checking Understanding:* In your opinion, the price of hiring an outside firm would be outrageous. What price do you think would justify farming the work out to them?

2. 14 – *Checking for Specifics:* What exactly does the accounting firm's service consist of?

    or – What is the cost difference between hiring someone to do the accounting internally compared to the cost of the outside firm?

3.   9 – *Obtaining Ideas:* What makes it not worth it?

    or – What price would be classified as outrageous?

Statement of Fact	Statement of Assumption
1. Can only be made after observation	1. Can be made anytime . . . before, during, or after the event
2. Stays with what can be observed	2. Goes beyond observation
3. Approaches certainty	3. Low or high degree of probability
4. Limited number	4. Unlimited number
5. Leads to agreement	5. Leads to disagreement
6. Things we observe going on around us	6. What we add to our observations and take for granted as fact

FIGURE 6.3
Differences between fact and assumption.

who's right. The questions on pages 153–155 would be useful in this kind of situation.

When a person expresses opinions without bothering to get the facts or supporting evidence, people begin to discount what that person says. Although acquiring facts can improve one's credibility, people seem to think that getting the facts is too time-consuming or that there is no need to do so.

The summary of what facts and assumptions contain, shown in Figure 6.3, can serve as a guideline.

Evaluating ideas and opinions on their own merit, rather than from a biased generalization, helps establish understanding and decreases distortions and misinterpretations. For instance, people often generalize from a single situation:

> "Customers don't want to pay top price, they're only interested in the cheapest product available."
> "I can't speak up to people and tell them now I feel because they'll get angry with me."
> "College graduates wouldn't last long in that routine job. We had one in our office and . . . ."

Such statements indicate that some things are that way but ignore all the rest. Because one person behaves in a certain way doesn't mean that *all* people will do so under the same circumstances. A person who frequently speaks in this manner can lose a certain amount of creditability in the eyes of those he works with. What we say and how we say it tells others just who and what we are.

You can increase your ability to get others to listen to you and reduce the generalizations and subjectivity in the ideas you present by asking yourself the following questions:

How much?
How often?
When?
Where?
As compared to what?

These questions will help you zero in on specifics, comparisons, and facts. Being a person who asks thought-provoking questions, defines terms, explores alternatives, and suspends judgment until you have the facts will go a long way in influencing people to listen to you.

DESCRIBING BEHAVIOR

Another area where talkers can get others to listen to them is in situations in which the talker discussing the performance of the other person such as performance appraisals, on-the-job training, discipline, making

Do's	Don'ts
• Be in the "OK–OK" attitude.	• Make the other person "not OK."
• Stay with what a person *does*.	• Make comments on what you imagine a person is.
Example: "You interrupted the customer."	*Example:* "You were rude to the customer."
• Use adverbs that relate to specific actions.	• Use adjectives that relate to labeling characteristics.
Example: "He talked loudly in the meeting."	*Example:* "He is a loudmouth."
• Describe what has occurred.	• Use labels that judge what happened.
Example: "When we don't agree on a problem-solving approach, the problem probably won't get resolved."	*Example:* "I can't believe how stubborn you can be."

FIGURE 6.4

Do's and don'ts of describing behavior.

criticism, and expressing negative feelings. How one person confronts another about behavior that is causing difficulty can affect the listener adversely, or it can bring about improvement. The major factors are the attitude of the talker, the choice of words, and the nonverbal elements of the message.

Often in these situations, the talker uses words and phrases that come across to the listeners as if they are being judged, condemned, or blamed unjustly for what has happened. Supervisors often express concern over the difficulty they have in expressing their negative feelings, stating limits, and criticizing without demoralizing the employee. On the other hand, numerous employees complain about the negative way in which they are dealt with during such situations.

For instance, a supervisor who isn't aware of the effect of the choice of words, the attitude, and the nonverbal behavior that are communicated during performance appraisal time can have a long-term detrimental effect on an employee's performance.

One way to handle such situations is to describe behavior, rather than to label it. The do's and don'ts in Figure 6.4 can be used as a guide.

EXERCISE 6.4

This exercise provides the opportunity to sharpen your ability to describe behavior. Using the preceding criteria as a model, change the statements that follow so that they are stated in specific, observable terms without labels.

1. "Keith, you're too pushy."

2. "Stan, your salespeople always want to be the center of attention."

3. "Sally, you're just trying to show Geri up."

4. "Rick, you're being stubborn."

EXERCISE 6.4
(continued)

5. "Sue, you're a slowpoke."

6. "Carlos, you're rude."

Possible Answers

1. "Keith, you've stated to me what you want three times now."

2. "Stan, your salespeople talked more than the others on this topic."

3. "Sally, you've taken the opposite point of view on nearly every change Geri has suggested."

4. "Rick, you seem to think this is the only way to handle the situation."

5. "Sue, when you do your work at this speed, it doesn't get done."

6. "Carlos, you've interrupted me three times during our discussion."

To further sharpen your skills in identifying description versus judgmental statements, read each sentence and determine if it is:

a. A description (D) or a judgment (J)

b. A general (G) or specific (S)

	Description or Judgment	General or Specific
1. Steve stopped talking after Joe said to him, "You're being ridiculous."	_____	_____
2. "Keith is too pushy."	_____	_____
3. "Carol is too emotional."	_____	_____
4. "That's the third time you've finished what I was going to say."	_____	_____
5. "It isn't right for Dennis to hog the boss's attention."	_____	_____
6. "You shouldn't have a negative attitude."	_____	_____
7. "Rick is being insensitive."	_____	_____

	Description or Judgment	General or Specific
8. "You were late two times this week."	_____	_____
9. "Cindy doesn't know how to think for herself."	_____	_____
10. "You finished that difficult assignment ahead of schedule."	_____	_____

Answers

1. D, S	3. J, G	5. J, G	7. J, G	9. J, G
2. J, G	4. D, S	6. J, G	8. D, S	10. D, S

AVOID ADVICE GIVING

Expressing ideas and information, rather than giving advice, is one way to stay out of the drama triangle and get others to listen to you. When we express our ideas and share information, we leave listeners free to decide for themselves. We then can use the idea and the information in light of their own goals, knowledge, and experience. Our advice is given based on our own beliefs and values, which might not fit the listener. In other words, it makes sense to us, but it might not make sense to the receiver.

Another variation of this phenomenon is focusing on exploring alternatives rather than answers and solutions. When we are quick to find answers, we don't give listeners the opportunity to explore for themselves what options are available. The more we focus on examining possible alternatives to reach a solution, the less likely we are to prematurely accept a quick solution. This quick solution may or may not fit a particular problem.

It is also important to express your ideas in terms of the value they may have for the listener, rather than the value or release the expression may provide for you. It's important to serve the needs of the listener. Watch out for information overload! When a listener is given too much information at one time, it can reduce the possibility that the person will effectively use the information received. When we give more than can be used, we are often satisfying some need of our own, rather than assisting the listener.

THE SHORTCOMINGS OF PRAISE

Another area in which the talker can influence the listener to listen is in the area of praise. For the most part, in our society we are taught that praise is positive, that individuals like receiving it.

You might be surprised to learn that praise is often experienced by the receiver as a negative. Feelings of discomfort, embarrassment, uneasiness, or defensiveness are felt. In an informal research study, I asked seminar participants to write down how they felt about being praised. Some comments were:

"When someone, especially my supervisor, praises me, I feel that an attempt is being made to manipulate me."
"I think inside my head, 'He's just saying that so I'll work harder.'"
"I wonder what she wants *now*."
"Embarrassment is what I feel; it's difficult to respond to."

Other responses to praise were vague denial or self-put-downs such as these:

"Well, I feel I do the best I can."
"OK, you're just saying that."
"I really can't take credit for it; Jane helped me, too."
"I like the way you do your work, too."

These people felt that praise was something to cope with, to be handled. When I asked why, they said it was because praise represents a threat, something they feel a need to defend against. They had correctly figured out that if someone judges positively, he or she can also judge negatively at another time. They knew that to judge implies superiority. Interestingly enough, some people responded angrily to praise when the praise didn't fit their self-image—"I am *not* a good cook."

Another unexpected factor was that when praise was absent in the worker's environment, it was sometimes interpreted as criticism—"He didn't say anything good about my work, so he must not like it."

The people in the study thought the following were the major characteristics of praise.

• Praise is a judgment; people can feel uncomfortable being judged.

• When we are judged, we can be found to be imperfect.

• Praise is any statement that makes a positive judgment about a person that contains very little additional information or meaning.

- Praise implies that the sender wants the receiver to change, and is trying to push him or her in a certain direction; people may want to change direction, but they don't want others to do it to them.

Although praise is often felt to be negative, the consensus of the people in the study was that it was better than nothing at all. The best response to work well done is nonjudgmental, positive feedback. All agreed that this type of response was very motivating. The major differences between the two approaches are shown in Figure 6.5.

EXERCISE 6.5

The following will help sharpen your ability to identify the difference between praise and nonjudgmental, positive feedback. Read each statement and determine if it is:

a. Praise (P)

b. A nonjudgmental, positive feedback (PF)

	Praise	Nonjudgmental Positive Feedback
1. "You're the nicest worker I have."	_____	_____
2. "You did your written project quickly and completely."	_____	_____
3. "Nice work."	_____	_____
4. "Thanks for getting your work done on time. It makes it easier for the rest of the team to get their jobs done."	_____	_____
5. "You're a good worker."	_____	_____
6. "I like the way you handled that difficult customer without getting angry."	_____	_____
7. "You're a kind and thoughtful person."	_____	_____
8. "I find your ability to summarize what has been said in our discussion very helpful."	_____	_____

Answers

1. P	3. P	5. P	7. P
2. PF	4. PF	6. PF	8. PF

Nonjudgmental, Positive Feedback	Praise
• A positive comment with meaning that specifically lets the listener know what the sender values	• A positive judgment with little additional meaning
• Specific, related to a task	• General and nonspecific
• A statement of observation and appreciation	• Value judgment, "right," "wise," "good," "nice"
• Identifies behavior, description of what the listener did	• Labels behavior, judgment of what the sender believed the listener did
• Rings true	• Can be taken as phony

FIGURE 6.5
Differences between positive feedback and praise.

Remember, stating positive feedback in nonjudgmental terms will influence the listener to be more open to what we are saying. Controlling what and how we express positive feedback will help impact the response we get from others.

SUMMARY

In this chapter, we have dealt with the factors that influence others to listen to us. We examined the effects that nonverbals have on the listener and explored an approach that can maximize their use. The fault-finding and the empathic attitudinal styles were described and compared, including the negative and positive impact each has on the listener. You were given an action-plan format to use for modifying behavior that doesn't serve you well. Guidelines for talkers were provided to help improve your ability to communicate more clearly. The meaning of any communication is shown by the response it elicits. Adjusting your verbal and nonverbal responses to what people say can help you get what you want.

To help you minimize distortions and mininterpretations, you learned the art of asking questions. The differences between facts and assumptions were examined, as well as the skill of describing behaviors. Both these tools will help you decrease the possibility of the listener being turned off and tuning out.

The important differences between praise and nonjudgmental, positive feedback were explored, so that you could increase your effectiveness in responding positively to people. Since people in general are seeking happiness, responding to them with effective, positive feedback can increase their pleasant experiences, thus influencing them subconsciously to listen to you.

SELF-TEST

1. Name three positive nonverbal behaviors:

Name three negative nonverbal behaviors:

2. There are six guidelines for talkers. Name one.

3. What is the value of asking questions?

4. What are the advantages of stating facts and not assumptions?

5. Why is describing behavior better than judging and blaming?

ANSWERS

1. Review your answers with those on pages 140–141, numbers 2, 3, 4, 5, 9, 10, 11, 13, 16, 20, 22, 27, and 30 for positive behaviors and the remainder for the negative ones.

2. Know what you want to say

   Know as much about the listener as possible

   Gain favorable attention—be aware of your nonverbal behavior

   Secure understanding

   Aid retention

   Encourage feedback

3. The value of asking questions is to

   • help minimize the chance of distortions and omissions.

   • make sure you understand what the talker means and clarify your understanding.

   • help keep a conversation going in a positive direction.

   • ensure you are dealing with facts and not assumptions.

   • encourage feedback and participation.

   • help the communication to be at level 1.

   • keep the discussion focused and decrease discussion going off on tangent.

4. Facts can be measured and lead to agreement. You will establish credibility, reduce disagreements, stay at level 1, solve problems more effectively. Assumptions lead to disagreement, decrease the possibility of others listening to us, and cause us to solve symptoms, not the real problem, so we lose a certain amount of standing in the eyes of others.

5. Describing behavior is better than judging because people don't like to judge. When they are judged, they tend to react by being defensive, justifying, or attacking. Describing helps the person see what they are doing without feeling condemned. When this happens, they are more likely to respond at level 1 so that the problem can be worked out.

7 Putting It All Together

God gave us two ears but only one mouth. Some people say that's because he wanted us to spend twice as much time listening as talking. Others claim it's because he knew listening was twice as hard as talking.

Unknown

Throughout this book, the harmful effects that ineffective listening habits can have on getting the job done efficiently and effectively have been emphasized. Communication breakdowns are being linked to people-problems ranging from low productivity to employee turnover, and to the failure of employees to carry out responsibilities. The stakes are extremely high in connection with poor listening. For instance, if each of America's 100 million or more workers made just one $5 mistake a year because of poor listening, the cost would be in excess of half a billion dollars.

A 1980 survey of the presidents of the Fortune's 1000 companies identified the most anxiety-producing work situations for top management. The failure of employees to accept or carry out responsibilities and the failure to get critical information were, by far, the first two choices. Both imply listening problems.[11]

PERCEPTIONS: WHAT THE MIND PERCEIVES

Effective listening often depends on what is going on in the head and heart of those communicating, rather than what is taking place on the outside. If we don't free our minds of perceptions and put aside our prejudices, our need to be right, and our preconceptions about those with whom we interact, it will be difficult to move from level 3 or 2 to level 1. One ingredient of the filter system that hinders a free-flowing communication process is the way the mind seems to work around our perceptions of others. The mind makes deductions that others will treat us as we treat them. If we are critical and judgmental of others, we reason that others are doing the same thing as they interact with us. Conversely, if we make a habit of extending acceptance, listening from the heart, admiration, and respect to others, we conclude that people are also extending these to us. Thus, we can create for ourselves a world that is either critical and hostile or one that is friendly and supportive.

Each time we make critical judgments of others, we create for ourselves a moment of unpleasantness and ugliness, for we instantly feel the effects of our own judgments, while the person we are judging will probably not even know about it. Even if the other person is aware of our judgment, it will still be up to that person to be affected by it. Therefore, the practices of judging others and refusing to accept them the way they are become self-defeating. To the extent that we allow others to be themselves, so will they allow us to be ourselves.

Yet another dimension of this process is that whenever we communicate, we are making public reports of our private perceptions. The response of others to what we say is feedback that tells us something about our perceptions. These responses are indicators that let us know how the communication is going and how our messages are being interpreted. Listening to the feedback of others allows us to modify what we are saying and correct any misunderstanding that may have arisen. In other words, each of these responses tells us something about the way we are heard by others, as well as something about our perceptions. It is when we are unaware observers that defective communication results.

Even though being aware of the responses of others, in the form of feedback to what we say, is extremely important to effective communication, we often ignore this feedback for various reasons:

"Sometimes I don't want to know what's going on because I don't know how to handle conflict."

"I want to avoid trouble, I like things to run smoothly."

"I know I'm in trouble if I listen and don't know how to handle criticism."

"I ignore the feedback in the hope that the problem will go away."

"I'm not good at handling people-problems."

While we are communicating with others, one way to "size them up" is by listening to what they say and how they say it. Often our appraisal of others tells us something about ourselves. Remember that judging others can be a dangerous thing, not so much because we may make a mistake about them, but because it may be revealing the truth about ourselves.

Knowing as much about people as possible allows you to be more effective in working with them. The better you are at reading people, the more you can predict how they will behave in certain circumstances. However, beware of making these predictions from judgments, preconceived ideas, or prejudices, rather than from observations that can be described and illustrated.

FIRST IMPRESSIONS

One area where "sizing up" a person can cause difficulty is when we meet someone for the first time. Such situations could occur when we have a new employee to supervise or work with, when we are calling on a new customer, or when we are a receptionist greeting new clients.

The danger lies in our retaining, out of our total experience, those things that fit into our frame of reference. This can result in letting our first impression rule what we listen to. When this impression is formed, we then only see what is consistent with this first impression. In fact, once we make a decision about someone, we work to prove that it's correct. Whatever quality we assign to that person initially, we tend to see and listen to what that person does to reinforce our first impressions. We unconsciously block other behaviors that don't support our impressions, in an effort to be right about understanding the person. When we listen at level 1 awareness of how this process operate within ourselves, we counteract this tendency; thus, we reduce resistance and build rapport.

A COMMUNICATION MODEL

The communication model in Figure 7.1[12] gives you a summary of the kinds of questions to keep in mind as a speaker and listener.

Typical Questions for the Talker to Keep in Mind	Typical Questions for the Listener to Keep in Mind
• Am I clear in my mind about what I want to say?	• What is the talker's intent—what does he or she want me to do?
• Am I using words and phrases to convey what is in my mind in such a way that my receiver will get the same picture?	• Am I listening actively—formulating my meaning and then checking back with the speaker to see if my meaning is his or her meaning?
• Am I getting meaningful feedback that tells me where my message is and isn't getting across?	• What information does the talker want me to have? What would be best for me to remember or take down?
• Am I aware of how I might be distorting information to reinforce my first impression?	• Am I resisting the feedback clues because I don't want to deal with the situation? If so, what can I do about it?
• Am I communicating in specific, observational terms and providing examples to illustrate what I mean?	• Am I sizing up the talker judgmentally? How is this affecting my interpretation of the message?
• Am I identifying my assumptions and opinions and keeping them separate from the facts?	• What barriers might be at work distorting the message?
• Am I keeping in mind the total impression I am creating, not just the words I am using?	• What questions could I ask to verify my understanding and minimize the effect of barriers?
• Am I remaining objective, or am I injecting too much of myself, my goals, my desires, etc.?	• What information is *not* being provided?
• Am I giving each point its due and helping my listener to understand them?	

FIGURE 7.1

A communication model: questions to keep in mind.

RESISTANCE

One way this information can be put together for your advantage is in the area of resistance. People often have difficulty dealing with resistance effectively. Those persons who have the widest range of responses and behaviors are more apt to be in control of the difficult situations they get involved in. In other words, if I am interacting with you in a different situation and am locked into old, programmed habits that influence me to behave automatically and compulsively, and if you have developed a wide range of responses and behaviors that allow you to behave from a mode of choice, you will have a greater influence on my behavior and the outcome than I would.

Avoid certain behaviors, words, and phrases when communicating with others because they have a tendency to turn the listener off, decrease the possibilities of being understood by the listener, and increase resistance. Behaviors such as putting people on the spot, coming from a know-it-all position, or looking down or sideways at the listener can cause the listener to look for an opportunity to get back at you, or to find ways of proving the talker wrong, thus building an environment of mistrust.

Words can be a source of trouble that builds resistance. Think of the effects the following words would have on the people at whom they are directed:

Worthless	Poor
Misconception	Weak
Unreasonable	Untrue
Inconsiderate	Rude
Thoughtless	Stupid
Unreliable	You never
Negligent	Slow
False	Impatient
Misled	Pushy
Serious mistake	Emotional

Words such as these build resistance and influence people not to cooperate or change their behavior, or else fail to be motivated.

EXERCISE 7.1

Following are some phrases that often turn people off and build resistance. Change the wording of the these phrases to that which you feel would be more acceptable to the receiver.

1. I can't accept the way you did this job.

2. If you actually did what you said . . .

3. You fail to see what I mean.

4. You misinterpreted my intention . . .

5. You neglected to get the information I asked you to get.

6. You are wrong in thinking that . . .

7. You didn't do this right.

EXERCISE 7.1
(continued)

Suggested Phrases in Place of the Preceding Ones

1. This work isn't completed the way we decided it was to be done. Let's review it.

2. When you did what you said, what was the outcome?

3. I don't think I conveyed to you the meaning I intended.

4. I think you have a different view of my intentions from what I meant them to be.

5. You didn't get the information I asked for. Perhaps I wasn't clear.

6. Let me clarify my reasons for doing the job this way.

7. This wasn't completed in the format I requested.

Whenever possible, choose words and phrases that have the least negative impact on the receiver. Since different words and phrases affect people differently, your choice of words is determined by who you are talking to and in what situation. When pointing out negative behavior in others, it's important to keep their self-esteem intact. It is also important to keep the focus of the communication centered on the problem, rather than on personalities; do not use such words as *thoughtless, unreasonable,* or *worthless.* Since we create impressions by the way we phrase our ideas, it is useful to pause and think through what we are about to say. Rambling statements can represent unclear thinking and influence the listener to become impatient for you to come to the point. Concise statements that deal directly with the issue have a greater chance of being listened to and accurately understood.

Disagreement often happens when the listener thinks he is right, based on how he interprets what you are saying. Recognize that disagreement in discussions is normal and inevitable. Prepare for it, and become more aware of the various aspects of the discussion.

GUIDELINES FOR LESSENING RESISTANCE

1. Ask for clarification or additional information to support what the person said instead of abruptly disapproving or contradicting what was said.

2. Find a point of agreement to build on, rather than disagreeing. If

you aren't able to find something in the content of the discussion, agree with the feelings that person is feeling—"I can understand your feelings of frustration when you aren't able to find a solution that works."

3. Control your own natural ego-building desire to get the upper hand by showing up weaknesses in the other's point of view. Do question the points that are not supported by examples or facts when you notice them, but do so in a way that keeps the other's ego and self-esteem intact.

4. Use every opportunity to positively reinforce the other person's behavior, ideas, or actions.

5. To get your instructions carried out and reach your goals that involve others, it's important to keep in mind that people want positive attention paid to what they say and do. They want understanding and clarity on what is expected of them, along with acceptance of themselves and their ideas whenever possible.

6. Very rarely will anyone change his or her mind by being asked, told, or directed to do so. If you want to influence the listener to see things differently, avoid using threatening language, both verbal and nonverbal. By so doing, you can decrease the need for the listener to defend himself.

7. Anticipate the things that would influence the listener to resist; take them into account, empathize, and know the other person. You can get to know others by:
   • Being aware of their beliefs—how do they look at the world?
   • What makes them feel comfortable, confident?
   • What throws them off balance?
   • What kind of phrases will help you get through to them?
   • What things do they do that are effective or ineffective?

8. People resist others less and listen to them more because of credibility. Whenever possible, build your credibility through the following means:
   a. Competence—how much do you know, how much experience do you have, and how well-trained are you?
   b. Knowledgeable—do you keep abreast of what is going on and pass the information on to others?
   c. Dependable and trustworthy—how much can you be trusted

to do what's in other people's interest: Are you sincere and honest, do you keep your word and not make promises you can't keep? If in an authority position, do you back your people, remain empathetic, and see things as others see them?

d. Energy and drive—do you have the drive to see things through and do what you say you will? Do you get the job done?

9. Stay at level 1 and be in the "OK–OK" attitude.

REDUCING RESISTANCE IN CONFRONTATION SITUATIONS: THE I-RATIONAL VERSUS YOU-BLAMING APPROACH[13]

It is important to let others know our limits and expectations if we want our relationships to run smoothly. Just as important is being able to express our negative feelings when we are upset about something. The manner in which we handle these situations will strongly influence the results. An *I-rational approach* can decrease resistance and increase the possibilities of the receiver listening to us. We most often confront people using a *you-blaming approach* that we learned during our socialization process. This you-blaming approach often builds resistance and turns people off. As a result, the listener tunes us out and very little of our message is heard and understood.

To understand the differences between the two approaches, study the comparison summary on page 177.

I-Rational Statement Guidelines

Now that you have examined the two methods and have an idea of what is meant by an I-rational approach, develop an I-rational statement. You may want to develop one concerning someone you already confronted if it didn't go well and you want to confront them again, your goal being to resolve the issue using the I-rational approach. You might have a situation you have been wanting to confront but didn't because you didn't know quite how to say it. Follow the guidelines described below.

An I-rational statement is a way to tell another person about a problem you are having with that person's behavior. The statement is to be expressed in a nonblaming manner. In addition, review the guidelines for

I-Rational Approach	You-Blaming Approach
1. This approach leads to a win/win resolution, both people feeling the solution meets their needs.	1. This approach usually leads to a win/lose resolution, one person feeling victorious, the other defeated.
2. A plan of action is developed to achieve the best outcome.	2. A plan of action is usually not developed.
3. One person discloses something he or she is unhappy about, in the hopes of modifying the other's and his or her behavior by problem solving.	3. One person discloses something the person is unhappy about to let the other know he or she *should* change.
4. The person is operating from an "OK–OK" frame of reference.	4. The person is operating from a "not-OK" frame of reference.
5. Confronting that is rational, objective, and not overly emotional	5. Confronting that is overly emotional and dumps feelings
6. The person is aware of his or her nonverbal behavior and the nonverbal clues the other person is sending, such as gestures, posture, facial expression, and tone of voice.	6. The person is not aware of the importance of the nonverbal aspects of the communication process.
7. States message in a nonblaming, noncritical manner—no put-downs	7. States message in a blaming, critical, judgmental manner, by name-calling, by stereotyping, or by attacking or threatening
8. Takes responsibility for his or her own feelings: "I feel upset . . ."	8. Puts the responsibility for his or her own feelings on the other person: "You make me upset . . ."
9. Allows the other person freedom of choice to change or not to change his or her behavior—no hidden *should, must,* or *ought to*	9. Doesn't allow freedom of choice—*should, must,* or *ought to* implied nonverbally
10. Observes and states specifically the behavior that is bugging him or her	10. Labels the behavior as good or bad, right or wrong
11. Doesn't use words that tend to push the other's hot buttons	11. Uses words that tend to push the other's hot buttons such as *you should, ought to, have to, must, are supposed to, never, always, all the time*

lessening resistance on pages 174–176. You will want to apply these guidelines as you work through the issue you are addressing.

EXERCISE 7.2

Take some time to think about this problem and the other person's behavior. Fill in the table below with information about the problem by describing what the person does, state your feelings about the behavior and then list the results and/or impact the behavior has on you, the relationship, and/or others. It is extremely important that the results and/or impact are those the other person values, cares about, or is interested in. As an example: people care about, or value, or are interested in:

- Credibility
- Improved productivity
- Saving time
- Team building
- Doing a good job
- Getting things done on time
- Relationships
- A promotion

- Morale
- Higher wages, greater commissions
- Personal, team, departmental, company image
- Being reliable, responsible
- Improved self-esteem, empowerment

It's important that your results and/or impact be expressed concisely in specific terms. Avoid generalization such as, "You always" or "You never." You can be sure the person will reply, "Yes, but you . . ." by finding a time in the last ten years when they did or didn't do what you said. If at all possible, your results and impact should be measurable.

Nonblaming Description of His/Her Behavior	My Feelings or Emotions	Results/Impact

PUTTING IT TOGETHER: Using the information that you noted on the previous page, write a concise, descriptive, I-rational statement.

"When you _____

(nonblaming description of other's behavior)

I feel _____ because _____

(feelings)

_____."

(results/impact)

You'll notice that the person using the I-rational approach has some awareness of the dynamics of the interaction with others. This is done by observing what is going on, using nonthreatening labeling words, being aware of the nonverbals and hot buttons, and stating specifics. On the other hand, the person using the you-blaming approach, by his or her very actions, is not aware of the negative impact he or she is having on the other person.

You've probably experienced numerous situations in which the you-blaming approach was used on you, and as a consequence you felt frustrated, put down, or angry. I can't stress enough the importance of using this I-rational approach as a method of decreasing resistance and reducing conflict.

Figure 7.2 provides examples of both statements. This will give you an idea of the differences in the approaches, along with a feeling about their possible impact on people.

EXERCISE 7.3

As additional practice, change the following you-blame statements so that they are expressed as I-rational statements.

Situation: Someone in the office has parked in your reserved space.
You-blaming statement: "You're not being very considerate of me. You know that is my space, not yours. Why don't you park in your own space as you're supposed to?"

I-rational statement:

EXERCISE 7.3
(continued)

Situation: A co-worker left early without letting you know.
You-blaming statement: "You left early *again,* leaving me swamped with work. The least you could have done is tell me about your plans."

I-rational statement:

Situation: A worker from another department doesn't return your phone calls.
You-blaming statement: "If you weren't so disorganized you'd see my phone messages on your desk. It's really annoying to have to call you three or four times to get the information I need from you."

I-rational statement:

Compare your I-rational statements with those that follow. If your statements differ, that's all right, because we all have our own style and use of language. However, it is important that your statements follow the ground rules for the I-rational approach noted on page 177.

I-rational statement: "I get irritated when I go to park in my reserved parking space and find out you are parked there. Since you know this is my space, I'd like your reasons for parking there."

I-rational statement: "I get upset when you don't let me know you are planning to leave early because I could have gotten someone else to help me out so I wouldn't be swamped with work at the end of the day."

I-rational statement: "Getting my phone calls returned by you is important to me because it means the project we are working on will be delayed, and the mutually established deadline could be missed."

I-Rational Statement	You-Blaming Statement
• I'm concerned that my last three reports were not completed by the due date because it lowers our creditability with the other departments.	• You never get my reports done on time because you're always talking on the phone.
• I feel uneasy when you don't include me in decisions that involve me, because these kinds of decisions are my responsibility.	• You hurt my feelings when you never include me in the decisions that I am involved in.
• I feel embarrassed when you criticize me in front of my co-workers because it is degrading to me.	• You embarrass me when you always criticize me in front of the other employees.
• When you leave the office without telling me, I feel frustrated because when someone calls I am not able to answer their questions directly and honestly.	• I can't tell people where you are because you never tell me where you're going.
• I'm concerned when you call me early in the morning to chat about personal matters because it results in my being late for work.	• You upset me when you always call me in the morning about personal matters because you make me late for work.
• I expect you to get your work done when you tell me you'll have it completed.	• You never get your work done on time.
• I expect you to follow my directions as I state them. To assist us both in checking understanding, I'd like you to restate what I ask you to do.	• I have all this work to do because you misunderstand what I say and botch things up.
• When you come to me with a complaint about a problem, I want you to have thought of a way to solve the problem so we can explore alternative solutions and develop a plan of action.	• You're always complaining about something.

FIGURE 7.2

Examples of
I-Rational versus
You-Blaming
statements.

CHANGE PROCESS

You have completed various exercises throughout this book, with the intent of improving your listening skills and modifying your listening habits. Change can happen quickly or at a snail's pace. Often, people resist change because they are uncertain as to the results they will get. New behavior can take some time to be internalized. Once you are aware of how the change process works and have a better understanding of its dynamics, you will be able to approach change more positively. The model shown in Figure 7.3 consists of a four-step process for integrating and internalizing a new behavior or skill so that the behavior or skill eventually becomes part of your behavior pattern for improved effectiveness.

Internal Experience that Takes Place when Integrating a New Skill or Behavior

Resistance	Natural tendency to stay with what is familiar
Being unsure	When we start to apply new skills and behaviors, we can feel phony.
Assimilation	Feeling less phony and becoming comfortable with the new behavior and new skill
Transference	Applying behavior or skills learned in one setting over to another setting or situation
Integration	Automatically and unconsciously reproducing the new behavior or skill as a part of you

FIGURE 7.3
Change process model.

Step 1
Nonawareness
Unconscious of one's behavior that results in ineffectiveness

Step II
Awareness
Conscious of one's behavior that results in ineffectiveness

Step III
Internalizing
Consciously putting into practice the new behavior or skill

Step IV
Integrated
Unconsciously applying the new behavior or skill

PREPARE OTHERS FOR YOUR CHANGE

Some cautions are in order about changing behavior. When you decide to respond to people differently, it is important to let them know your intentions. It is also useful to modify your behavior gradually. Often, those around us feel threatened when our change happens in giant leaps. Share with your co-workers some of the behaviors you have found that interfere with your effectiveness and how you intend to modify those behaviors. Ask for your co-workers' support in making this transition from old behavior to new behavior.

I have found that certain practice efforts happen when the empathetic approach is used. People tell me that when they use this approach, they get several types of results.

Over the years, I have collected peoples' comments and found that the results fit into six categories. The following list of accomplishments reflects the results reported to me.

THE ACCOMPLISHMENTS THAT CAN BE GAINED THROUGH EMPATHETIC LISTENING

- Empathetic listening may solve the problems of other people. Giving people a chance to talk through their problems may clarify their thinking about the subject and provide the necessary emotional release.

- Empathetic listening can reduce tension. It gives others a chance to get their problems or viewpoints off their chests, clearing the air of tension and hostility.

- Empathetic listening facilitates cooperation. When people feel you are really interested in them and their problems, thoughts, and opinions, they respect you and will more readily cooperate with you.

- Empathetic listening promotes communication. In the business world, communication is essential for getting the job done correctly. Often, communication breaks down because neither party has learned to listen at level 1. Skillful listening has solved many communication problems.

- Empathetic listening develops an active mind. Real listening at level 1 is active. At this level, listeners are continually trying to understand the feelings behind the words of the speaker, keeping the mind active and attentive.

- Empathetic listening can enhance the self-concept. True listening assumes that other people have worth, dignity, and something to offer. This attitude makes others feel good about themselves.

SUMMARY

Throughout this book, I have emphasized several factors that affect listening habits and levels. Often, a step-by-step procedure can help put concepts in a logical sequence so that they can be more easily remembered. The following is such a system.

THE LISTENING SYSTEM

I. Examine your own listening patterns:
- Barriers and filters
- Socialization process

II. Determine what areas you would like to improve.

III. Improve your listening by remembering to
- create a positive atmosphere by being alert, attentive, nondistracted, and using nonverbal behavior effectively.
- be interested in the other person.
- be in an "OK–OK" position.
- have a spirit of cooperation.
- be a sounding board—allowing the sender to bounce ideas and feelings off of you nonjudgmentally and noncritically.
- remain "unhooked and neutral." Keep your anger and other emotions out of the interaction.
- facilitate the other person in problem solving.

IV. Establish and maintain the atmosphere and flow of the conversation by using these listening techniques:
- Clarify meaning and understanding.
- Check assumptions.
- Restate the person's basic idea, emphasizing facts.
- Reflect the person's feelings.
- Use noncommittal words and a positive tone of voice.
- Summarize major ideas and concepts.
- Encourage others to talk about problems and share ideas.

I have enjoyed sharing this information with you and wish each of you success in carrying out your plan of action for improved listening effectiveness.

SELF-TEST

1. List three things you learned about perceptions.

2. What is one thing you learned about resistance?

3. There were nine guidelines for lessening resistance. What is the guideline you found most useful?

4. Name three things that are different between the I-rational approach and the you-blaming approach.

1. Your list of three things could have included the following:

   • Preconceptions can keep us at level 2 or 3.

   • How we perceive others if often a reflection of ourselves.

   • Judgments are part of negative perceptions that can lead to self-defeating behavior.

   • When we communicate, we make public our private perceptions.

   • People size us up by what we say and how we behave, which is the effect of our perceptions.

   • It is important to be aware of our perceptions so that we can modify them if necessary.

2. Please review pages 172–177 to check the choice you made.

3. Check your answers with the guidelines on pages 174–176.

4. The differences between the two approaches are on page 177. Check your answers with the information on that page.

Notes

1. From studies summarized by Dr. Ralph Nichols in his book, *Are You Listening?* (New York: McGraw-Hill), 1957.
2. Robert Watson and Henry Clay Lindgren, *Psychology of the Child* (New York: John Wiley & Sons, Inc.), 1973.
3. Reprinted with permission from the Associated Press.
4. Adopted from Dr. Stephan B. Karpman's article, "Fairy Tales and Script Drama Analysis," *Transactional Analysis Bulletin* D11, No. 26, April 1968, pp. 39–43.
5. Adapted from Joseph Luft and Harry Ingham's Johari Window presentation (1955) and later in *Group Process: An Introduction to Group Dynamics* by Joseph Luft (Palo Alto: National Press Books), 1970.
6. "Communication Without Words," *Psychology Today* September 1968, p. 53.
7. "Nonverbal Communication: Exploration into Time, Space, Action, and Object," *Dimensions in Communication,* ed. James Campbell and Hall Hepner (Belmont, CA: Wadsworth), 1970, p. 258.
8. *The Farther Reaches of Human Nature* (New York: Viking Press), 1960, pp. 70–71.
9. Patricia A. Muller, M.A.R.N., in *Supervisor Nurse* April 1980.
10. Dr. Scott Parry, *The Art of Asking Questions* (Princeton, N.J.: Training House, Inc.), modified version, reprinted by permission.
11. Susan Mundale, "Why More CEOs Are Mandating Listening and Writing Training," *Training Magazine* October 1980.
12. "Listening: Sharpening Your Analytical Skills," a self-paced program by Training House, Princeton Junction, N.J., 1981.
13. Adapted from Dr. Thomas Gordon's *Parent Effectiveness Training* (New York: Peter H. Wyden, Inc.), 1970.

Suggested Reading

Autry, James, *Life and Work—A Manager's Search for Meaning,* William Morrow & Co., New York, 1994.

Axtell, Roger E., *Gestures,* John Wiley & Sons, New York, 1991.

Bradshaw, John, *Creating Love,* Bantam Books, Pittsburg, PA, 1992.

Broadwell, Martin M., *The New Supervisor,* Addison-Wesley, Reading, MA, 1990.

Burley-Allen, Madelyn, *Managing Assertively,* John Wiley & Sons, New York, 1982.

Buscoglia, Leo F., Ph.D., *Personhood—Art of Being Fully Human,* Fawcett Columbine Publishing, New York, 1982.

Canfield, Jack, Hansen, Mark, and Victor Hansen, *Chicken Soup for the Soul,* Health Communications, Inc., Deerfield Beach, FL, 1993.

Covey, Stephen R., *The 7 Habits of Highly Effective People,* Simon and Schuster, New York, 1990.

Creech, Bill, *The Five Pillars of TQM,* Dutton Publishing, New York, 1994.

Dyer, Wayne W., Dr., *Real Magic,* Harper, New York, 1992.

Fanning, Patrick, *Visualization for Change,* New Harbinger Publications, Inc., Oakland, CA, 1988.

Johnson, Spencer, M.D., *Yes or No—The Guide to Better Decisions,* HarperCollins, New York, 1992.

Kaile, Earl, *Listening—A Way of Becoming,* Regency Books, Waco, TX, 1977.

Meiss, Ron, *Effective Listening Skills,* Career Tracks Publishers, Boulder, CO, 1991.

Peters, Tom, *Thriving on Chaos,* Harper Perennial, New York, 1987.

Rubin, Theodore Isaac, M.D., *Real Love—What It Is and How To Find It,* Continuum Publishers, New York, 1990.

Slesinski, Raymond A., *Skyrocket Your Sales,* Pelican Publishing Co., Gretna, LA, 1986.

Walther George R., *Upside-Down Marketing,* McGraw-Hill, New York, 1994.

Index